WATERSIDE WALKS
In Somerset

G000268741

Charles Whynne-Hammond

COUNTRYSIDE BOOKS
NEWBURY, BERKSHIRE

First published 2000
© Charles Whynne-Hammond 2000

COUNTRYSIDE BOOKS
3 Catherine Road
Newbury, Berkshire

To view our complete range of books,
please visit us at
www.countrysidebooks.co.uk

ISBN 1 85306 624 9

Designed by Graham Whiteman
Cover illustration by Colin Doggett
Line illustrations by Trevor Yorke
Photographs by the author
Maps by Glenys Jones

Produced through MRM Associates Ltd., Reading
Printed by Woolnough Bookbinding Ltd., Irthlingborough

Contents

Area Map Showing Location of the Walks

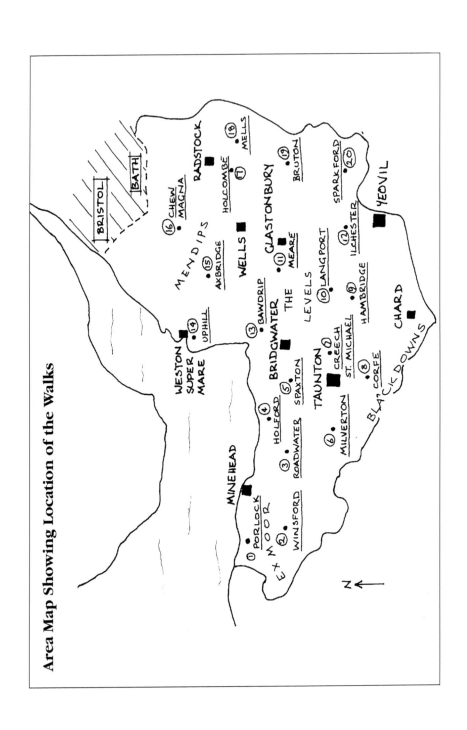

Walk

Publisher's Note

We hope that you obtain considerable enjoyment from this book; great care has been taken in its preparation. Although at the time of publication all routes followed public rights of way or permitted paths, diversion orders can be made and permissions withdrawn.

We cannot, of course, be held responsible for such diversion orders and any inaccuracies in the text which result from these or any other changes to the routes nor any damage which might result from walkers trespassing on private property. We are anxious though that all details covering the walks are kept up to date and would therefore welcome information from readers which would be relevant to future editions.

INTRODUCTION

Somerset is, perhaps, one of the most varied counties in England and one of the most beautiful in which to follow a waterside walk. From the high moorlands of Exmoor in the west, towards the Devon border, to the chalk downlands in the east, that stretch into Wiltshire, the landscape changes constantly. In the north, around Bristol and Bath, the Mendip Hills offer the well-known features of limestone scenery, with barren pastures, caves and gorges. In the south the Blackdown Hills, Windwistle and the Hamstone range near Yeovil produce a pretty countryside of steep slopes, woodlands and dense hedgerows. At the centre of the county are the Somerset Levels – a wetland paradise for birds where the broad fens are broken by a number of curious hillocks such as Brent Knoll and the mystical Glastonbury Tor.

Water is such a pleasant companion on a walk and there is an abundance of water here. There are lakes and reservoirs, meandering rivers, fast moorland streams, historic canals and straight drainage channels. The 20 walks in this book, which vary in length between 2½ and 6 miles, have been carefully chosen to give the widest possible range of scenery and waterway. They include the rivers Exe, Brue, Parrett, Yeo, Chew, Cam and Mells; the expansive reservoirs at Cheddar and Hawkridge; the King's Sedgemoor Drain; and two canals. There are wide views out over the Bristol Channel, but in general these walks take you into the heart of Somerset's peaceful and beautiful countryside, and the coastline itself is not explored.

Each walk in this book is accompanied by a description of the immediate locality, putting the landscape in its historical and geographic context, together with suggestions for parking and refreshments. All the walks have at least one pub close at hand. At the end of each chapter some places of interest nearby are listed, for those wishing to explore the areas more fully. The sketch maps should be sufficient to help with route-finding but the relevant OS maps are recommended for further detail or for devising alternative routes. Walkers are reminded always to wear suitable footwear and carry waterproofs.

Finally, I should like to thank Glenys Jones for drawing the sketch maps and Gwen Cassell for helping with the final draft.

Charles Whynne-Hammond

WALK 1

HAWK COMBE AND PORLOCK

This breathtaking walk follows one of the wooded combes that can be reached from Porlock, a pretty little town close to the coast. It accompanies the Hawk stream up towards the combe head and returns at a higher level along the top of the wooded valley side. Towards the end of the route there are some splendid views across the Bristol Channel and over Porlock to Selworthy Beacon. The route is very clear but some steep gradients must be negotiated.

Hawk Combe

The uplands of west Somerset, which stretch into Devon, are made of old red sandstone. They rise to 1,700 feet and are drained by a number of rivers, including the Exe, Barle, Quarme and Lyn. This is a largely unspoilt region, of moorlands, high pastures and deep wooded combes. Much of it forms part of the Exmoor National Park, and should not be missed by the tourist or rambler. Porlock would be a perfect base for many days of walking and exploring. Footpaths run out in all directions: down to the coast; across the meadows to Selworthy

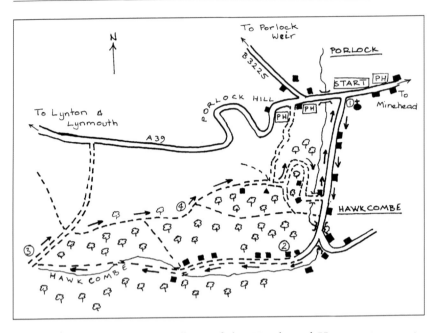

Beacon; inland along the valleys of the Hawk and Horner streams to the Exmoor hilltops. Dunkery Beacon, at 1,704 feet the highest point in the National Park, is only 4 miles to the south. In addition there are numerous picturesque villages to discover, within easy reach: Allerford with its thatched cottages and old packhorse bridge; Selworthy, the famous National Trust hamlet; Oare, the scene of the shooting incident in Blackmore's novel *Lorna Doone*. Porlock itself should also be explored, with its thatched cottages, its interesting church dating back to the 13th century, and its little museum housed in the handsome 15th century Doverhay. Less than 2 miles away is picturesque Porlock Weir, where a cluster of buildings surrounds a little harbour.

There are several pubs and teashops in Porlock, all offering a wide selection of food and drink. The Ship Inn (telephone: 01643 862507) stands at the bottom of Porlock Hill. This is one of the oldest and most famous pubs on Exmoor. Not far away, along the High Street, is the Royal Oak. Very popular both with locals and walkers, it has low beamed ceilings, old pictures around the walls and a friendly atmosphere. Regular menu cards and daily specials offer everything from sandwiches to main courses and real ales like Boddingtons are served. It is also open all day and advertises morning coffee, cream teas and even take-aways. Telephone: 01643 862798.

- **HOW TO GET THERE:** Porlock is 6 miles west of Minehead on the A39 road to Lynton and Lynmouth. It can also be reached from across the moor, the road from Exford joining the A39 west of Porlock Hill.
- **PARKING:** There are many car parks in Porlock, but the town can be busy in summer. Other parking spaces may be found down Parsons Street (southwards) and Villes Lane (eastwards).
- **LENGTH OF THE WALK:** 6 miles. Map: OS Landranger 181 Minehead and Brendon Hills (GR 886467).

THE WALK

1. Walk down Parsons Street, beside the church of St Dubricius with its curiously truncated spire, a sad result of a great storm in the early 18th century. This road goes south through that part of Porlock called Hawkcombe, where there are many interesting and pretty cottages. Continue all the way to the end. Already the little Hawk stream is beside you and the route is aiming up the combe ahead. In due course you reach a point where the lane bends left and crosses the stream. Keep straight on here, along the lane marked by a dead-end signpost, indicating that the public road stops after 150 yards. There is also a bridleway sign here, pointing to Hawkcombe Head. Walk past the pretty rows of cottages to where the tarmac ends. Continue straight on.

2. The route upstream along the bottom of Hawkcombe is clear and needs little detailed description. At first you follow a clear gravel track with the stream to your left. There are several houses and cottages dotted about the valley and this trackway serves them all. But this stretch is pleasant nevertheless, since the woodlands provide a screen and shelter from any residential activity. Beyond the last of the houses the track becomes more of a path and you are alone with the trees. After crossing the stream a couple of times by footbridge you soon reach a gateway. Through this is Hawkcombe Woodland, 250 acres of ancient oak woods owned by the National Park Authority. An information board stands beside the gate. Continue up the combe keeping the stream close to your left and ignoring all other paths. Eventually, after passing a lonely wooden barn and gaining height as you walk upstream, you meet a main trackway. Turn right along it.

3. This wide trackway leads you steeply uphill, to climb the valley side at an angle. At the top, on the edge of the woodland, is a footpath

Porlock Bay

signpost. Left would take you to Whitstone Post. The right is named as North Terrace Path, and this is the direction to follow. Once again, the route is clear. The well-trodden footpath contours along the top of the valley slope, close to the edge of the woodland. Beyond a gate there is a fork. Ignore the right descent and keep left to maintain height. Where the trees thin out a pleasant view can be enjoyed across the combe. A lovely stretch indeed, so take your time. Soon the path swings left to reach a gate at the edge of the wood. A choice now presents itself, indicated by a footpath signpost.

4. To the right a path descends through the woodland, offering a fairly direct route back to Hawkcombe. Straight on, through the gateway, a bridleway leads across farmland to reach Hawkcombe by a slightly more circuitous route. The latter option should be chosen if you would like to enjoy a wonderful view. The bridleway runs along the edges of two fields, beside a hedgebank. It then descends past a house and radio aerial, by way of a deeply-cut gully below some trees. Bearing right at the fork it then curves down to an apparent dead-end. At this point go through the high wire gate on the left and continue the descent down to Parsons Street. But this last stretch of the route should not be hurried. The view from the top, which is Porlock Hill, is spectacular. Porlock Bay lies below. Ahead is the great mass of Selworthy Beacon; to the left on a clear day is Wales. Return down Parsons Street to the start.

PLACES OF INTEREST NEARBY

Near Allerford (2 miles east) is the *Exmoor Falconry and Animal Farm* (telephone: 01643 862816) whilst at *Minehead* (6 miles east) are numerous tourist attractions including Butlins Somerwest World, the Aquasplash Leisure Centre and the northern terminal of the West Somerset Steam Railway.

WALK 2

THE RIVER EXE AT WINSFORD

Winsford is the perfect base from which to explore the Exe valley and this walk follows the river upstream towards Exford, returning along a grassy bridleway and field paths with splendid views down the valley. Throughout its course, and especially in its Exmoor section, the Exe is a clear and unpolluted waterway, its valley steep-sided and wonderfully unspoilt.

Exmoor is both bleak and beautiful. It is also rich in wildlife, archaeology and legend. On the moorlands and in the beech and oak woodlands there are red deer, wild ponies and healthy populations of foxes and badgers. Ancient burial mounds and standing stones scatter the hills and there are many signs of old mineworkings, railway routes and mills. According to the author R.D. Blackmore the Doone family terrorised Exmoor in the 17th century, whilst today there remain stories of 'beasts' at large. The Exe rises on the remote plateau called 'The Chains', an upland bog close to the Devon border south of Lynton and Lynmouth. Winsford is about 12 miles downstream from the source, by which time the river is wide and fast-flowing. But there is still a long journey ahead for these waters. The Exe winds attractively through

12

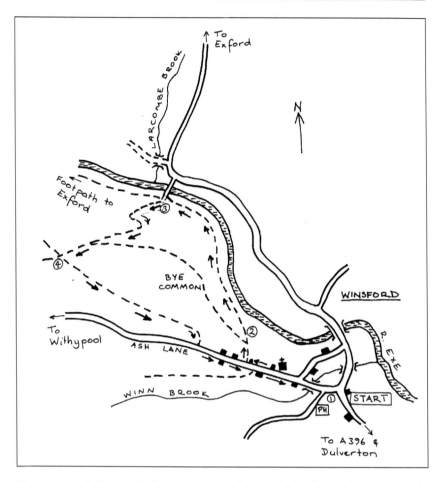

Tiverton and Exeter before reaching the English Channel at Exmouth. Winsford itself is a pretty little place with many thatched cottages, a number of little stone bridges, a ford and, standing above the rooftops, a handsome 15th century church. Ernest Bevin, the famous Labour politician, was born in the village in 1881.

Close to the ford are the Bridge Cottage tea rooms, with tables and chairs laid out in the gardens. Nearby is the Royal Oak, which has been called the prettiest pub on Exmoor. This should not be missed. With a wonderfully traditional ambience, complete with low beamed ceilings, many small bar rooms, old pictures hanging on the walls and wooden furniture, the service is friendly and welcoming. There is a wide range of bar snacks and main meals whilst ever-changing daily specials are listed on blackboards. The real ales change also, but usually include such local brews as Exmoor and Cotleigh beers. Telephone: 01643 851455.

- **HOW TO GET THERE:** Winsford is 9 miles south-west of Minehead, 5 miles north of Dulverton. It can most easily be reached from the A396 road, or else from the B3223 across the moor.
- **PARKING:** Vehicles can be left at any reasonable space. There is a designated parking area near the village centre, opposite a motor repair garage.
- **LENGTH OF THE WALK:** 3½ miles. Map: OS Landranger 181 Minehead and Brendon Hills (GR 906349).

THE WALK

1. From the village centre road junction walk uphill along the road to Withypool, past the church of St Mary Magdalene. This road continues (as Ash Lane) past some detached bungalows and houses. Ignore the footpath signpost pointing left to Winsford Hill. This can be followed on another occasion! The route required for this circular walk begins a little further up on the right, just past the Winsford village signboard. A footpath fingerpost points to a track beyond a metal gate: 'Exford'. Follow this track downhill – a wide, clear earthy path descending the wooded valley side. After about 200 yards there is a fork and another signpost. Left (uphill) goes to Exford via Bye Common; right (downhill) goes to Exford via Larcombe. Follow the latter, thus descending gradually to the riverbank.

2. For the next mile the route needs little description. Continue along the bottom of the Exe valley keeping fairly close to the river's edge. There is a gate to go through, on the way, but the path is clear throughout, as it winds between the trees. This is a lovely stretch, the river making a fine companion as it bubbles along. There is a road on the far bank but this can hardly be seen or heard and so fails to detract from the pleasure of the stroll. In due course you reach a gate onto a main track. There is a footpath signpost here. To the right is a bridge across the river to the road. To the left is a bridleway to Exford along the riverbank. To the sharp left is a bridleway to Ash Lane. Follow this last one.

3. The track required begins on the far side of another gate and climbs steadily up the valley side. It is a wide, grassy path that ascends the slope at an angle. Half way up it kinks left then right. During the necessary stops to regain breath you can admire the view down and along the Exe valley. Continue to the top (going through another gateway on the way) and where the track peters out at the summit, walk across the grass in the same direction until you reach a lone footpath signpost. Now follow the route, back left, signposted to Winsford via Ash Lane.

4. Keeping the hedgerow to your right walk along the top edge of the field all the way to the far corner. Going through a gateway there continue beside the same hedgerow along the edge of the next field. Passing a sheep pen proceed to the bottom corner where there are two gates. Go through the right-hand one and follow the hedgerow downhill. The road is soon reached at the bottom. Turn left for the descent back to Winsford.

PLACES OF INTEREST NEARBY

At *Wimbleball Lake* (5 miles south-east) there are fishing, angling and rowing opportunities. This reservoir also has parking and picnic facilities dotted around its shore. The little town of *Dulverton* (5 miles south) has many old and interesting buildings together with a museum and a National Park Information Centre.

Winsford

THE WASHFORD RIVER AND ROADWATER

This interesting walk from Roadwater, with its fascinating mixture of properties, explores the lovely wooded Washford valley in the Brendon Hills. This area was once a hub of industrial activity but now stands quiet and half-forgotten. From Roman times until the 19th century iron ore was mined here and the landscape still shows the evidence. Country lanes and clear paths are used throughout, but there are two stretches where a steep ascent is required, the views making the effort worthwhile.

Roadwater

The uplands at the eastern end of the Exmoor National Park are called the Brendon Hills. They are made of the same rock as the Exmoor range, Devonian sandstone, but are lower, gentler and more wooded. The mining of iron ore reached its peak in the 19th century, when the Brendons supplied raw material for the South Wales steel factories. Ore was extracted from the ridge in the area around Goosemoor and taken by rail to the coast at Watchet. The journey involved the construction and use of an 'incline' from the top of the ridge to the Washford valley, a miraculous feat of engineering. Along the Washford valley a mineral line was built alongside the stream, through the village of Roadwater, which in consequence grew into a busy commercial settlement. This walk follows the course of the old mineral line, which has now been made into a peaceful, narrow tarmac-covered lane. It runs through an area that once bustled with activity. Those wishing to lengthen the route, and explore further the industrial archaeology of the district, can follow the Washford river all the way to the bottom of the 'incline' at Comberow.

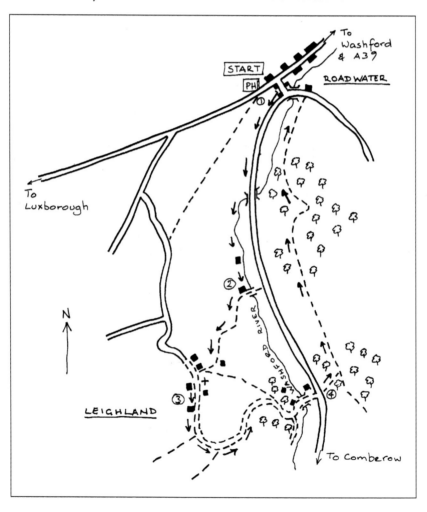

Roadwater is a long, narrow settlement stretching for more than a mile along the bottom of the wooded Washford valley. It has a fascinating mixture of old cottages and Victorian terraces; of picturesque farm buildings and modern commercial premises. At the northern end of the village is the Valiant Soldier inn. This very pleasant and friendly establishment has become popular with both walkers and those on motor tours or party outings. There is a large main bar room with a low beamed ceiling and walls well hung with brassware. Open fires and a large wooden dresser complete the traditional atmosphere. Exmoor Ales and Bass beers are served but it is the food offered that makes the place well-known. A large blackboard lists the tempting choice, with everything from bar snacks to such interesting main meals as stag and boar pie or spinach and blue cheese tortellini. There is a special 'Kids' menu and always a good range of fish and vegetarian meals. Telephone: 01984 640223.

- **HOW TO GET THERE:** Roadwater is 7 miles south-east of Minehead and can best be reached from the A39, turning south at Washford.
- **PARKING:** Vehicles can be left at various places along the village street, especially near the Valiant Soldier (which also has its own car park).
- **LENGTH OF THE WALK:** 3 miles. Map: OS Landranger 181 Minehead and Brendon Hills (GR 030382).

THE WALK

1. Turn left outside the pub and right at the first group of buildings reached. The lane required has a sign telling you that it narrows ahead to 9 feet, not surprisingly since it squeezes between some old cottages. At the next junction, where the road divides, turn right down the lane marked as a dead-end. The Washford river should now be on your left-hand side. This lane follows the course of the old mineral line and is the route required. After the first cottage you will notice that the stream is to the right, and so it remains for the next mile, passing in due course a small collection of pretty detached cottages. This is a lovely valley: woods either side and the high Brendon ridge ahead. Walk slowly and enjoy.

2. Leave the mineral mine route by turning right along a path marked as a bridleway to Leighland. This will be seen just after a large detached house and immediately before a long wire fence. After crossing the river you follow the path up the valley side. It is clear, being cut deeply into the bordering hedgebanks. By several bends it winds its way up to the road at Leighland hamlet. Here there is a farmstead, a few cottages and the handsome St Giles Chapel built in 1862. Turn left.

3. The lane that you are now following is marked as unsuitable for heavy goods vehicles. And so it is for it later degenerates from tarmac to earth and gravel. It is a pretty lane, however, with hedgerows either side and views ahead and down to the left across the Washford valley. Continue all the way as the lane descends back down to the river, ignoring all other footpaths signposted either side. Towards the bottom the way bends to the right, after which is a footpath signpost pointing left to Chidgley and Roadwater. Follow this track past some buildings, over the river and up to rejoin the mineral line lane. Another footpath sign awaits at the junction.

4. The easy way back to Roadwater is to turn left and follow the mineral line route along the riverbank. But this retraces much of the outward journey. A more attractive way back is to cross straight over

The Washford valley

the lane and follow the narrow footpath signposted to Chidgley. This climbs steeply up the valley side at an angle through a woodland. Half way up the slope this path joins a wide track that contours along. This is a bridleway. Turn left and follow it all the way back to Roadwater village. This is a very attractive stretch, with views much of the way, across the Washford valley and beyond. The route is very clear, even as it bends right and left, through two gates, as it crosses a side valley. At first, and later too, the track runs through woodland, whilst the middle section follows the top edge of a field. At the far end you join a road. Turn left to return to the Valiant Soldier.

PLACES OF INTEREST NEARBY

The little town of *Dunster* (4 miles north-west) should not be missed, with its picturesque main street, Butter Cross and National Trust-owned *Dunster Castle* (telephone: 01643 821314). At neighbouring Washford is the *Somerset and Dorset Railway Museum* (telephone: 01984 640869).

WALK 4

HODDER'S COMBE AND HOLFORD

The Quantock Hills, rising to more than 1,000 feet, offer an attractive landscape of heather and gorse moorlands cut by deep wooded valleys. It is a walkers' paradise boasting wonderful views, numerous archaeological remains, pretty villages and many fast-flowing streams where wildlife abounds. This walk follows one of these streams, up Hodder's Combe to its source on the high moorland ridge from where spectacular views can be enjoyed, across Exmoor and over towards Wales.

Hodder's Combe

Hodder's Combe is one of the many wooded valleys that dissect the Quantock ridge. Oak and beech trees densely cover the steep valley sides and the clear, bubbling waters echo in the rocky glens. Not surprisingly the poets Wordsworth and Coleridge (living for a while at Alfoxton and Nether Stowey respectively) were both much inspired by the surroundings. Holford, where the walk begins, is an attractive village with a small Norman church (much rebuilt in Victorian times)

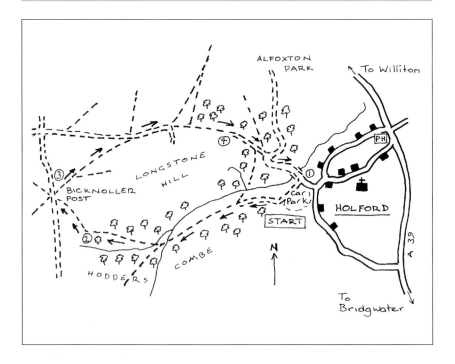

and a plethora of thatched cottages. It hides well its industrial past. During the Middle Ages cloth was made here (there were two fulling mills) and the 18th century saw the beginning of copper mining nearby. In the 19th century a large tannery was set up just south of the village, in a building now known as Combe House Hotel. Today most of the activity generated at Holford seems to revolve around walking, cycling and sightseeing. A car park has been created amongst the trees at the southern end, and here tourists tend to gather prior to their exploration of the surrounding countryside. The local National Trust Ranger is often based here, offering advice and guiding walking parties, and close by is a Youth Hostel.

There are many walks that can be enjoyed in this corner of Somerset and there is no shortage of watering holes. Here in Holford is the Plough, a most pleasant, friendly and popular establishment. A freehouse selling Flowers Original and local Exmoor ales, it offers a full range of bar snacks and main meals, served from a separate food bar. Daily specials are written up on a blackboard. The decor is truly traditional with low-beamed ceilings, wooden dado and walls hung with old photographs. Telephone: 01278 741232.

- **HOW TO GET THERE:** Holford stands on the A39 between Bridgwater (9 miles) and Minehead (16 miles). It is 2 miles inland from the Bristol Channel.
- **PARKING:** The village car park is signposted south of the church, round the corner off the lane that leads to the Youth Hostel. Parking space is limited elsewhere in Holford.
- **LENGTH OF THE WALK:** 4½ miles. Map: OS Landranger 181 Minehead and Brendon Hills (GR 155410).

THE WALK

1. The route begins along the trackway running between the Holford car park and Holford Bowling Green (which is actually a public amenity open space rather than a greensward for bowls). This trackway, signposted as a public bridleway, is wide, gravelled and runs beside a number of attractive cottages and gardens. After a short distance you enter a woodland, with a stream close by to your right. This is Hodder's Combe, and the walk upstream along the riverside path should not be rushed. The gravel track becomes a wide earthy path but the route is clear all the way. Ignore other paths that turn off, to climb the valley sides, and stay close to the main river. At one point you cross a tributary stream (by stepping stones). Soon after, you cross the main river (also by stepping stones) and continue up the combe, now with the river on your left. Eventually after gaining more height still, you emerge out of the woodland. Ahead and above are the bracken-clad slopes of the Quantock ridge.

2. As you leave the tree-line at the top of Hodder's Combe and the path climbs through the bracken, so Quantock's other landscape opens out. Heather starts to appear, and gorse too as you approach the skyline. And then comes the panorama! From the crest of the hills you can see (weather permitting) Taunton Vale on the left, the Brendon Hills and Minehead coastline ahead and over the sea to Wales on the right. As the gradient levels walk straight on to an old wooden post, standing some 5 feet above the moorland grass. This is Bicknoller Post, marking an ancient junction of trackways. The wide, red-earthed ridgeway track runs through here, an old drove road, and all around are the remains of ancient burial mounds. This is a spot for exploring and picnicking.

3. The way back begins along a grassy path that runs north-eastwards

The village pub at Holford

between the heather. Keep Minehead back over your left shoulder and the trees of Hodder's Combe over to your right. Ignore the first right fork (close to a heather-covered tumulus to the left) and walk straight on. The Bristol Channel should be ahead. In due course you drop down to join a wide earthy track, close to three small trees, lone and windswept. Bear right to follow this track eastwards, enjoying the sea views to your left all the way. Ignoring all other paths either side continue straight on, in due course passing a patch of woodland, which you should keep to your left.

4. The final descent, down to Holford, begins where the path divides. To the right the track bends back towards Hodder's Combe, down towards the trees. To the left (which you follow) the track runs downhill towards the distant coastal plain, where stands the much-criticised Hinkley Point Nuclear Power Station. This path soon becomes an attractive woodland track, running between the beech trees of Alfoxton Park, the estate which surrounds the Georgian mansion (now an hotel) which once boasted William Wordsworth as a tenant. Incidentally this trackway, which you have been following since the three lone and windswept trees, was the medieval main road linking Holford and West Quantoxhead, now superseded by the A39. Today it provides an extremely attractive walk back to the car-park, whence this circuit began.

PLACES OF INTEREST NEARBY

At Nether Stowey, 3 miles east of Holford, is *Coleridge's Cottage* (National Trust) where Samuel Taylor Coleridge lived 1797-99. It was here the poet wrote some of his most famous works (telephone: 01278 732662). Near Stogumber (5 miles south-west) is *The Bee World and Animal Centre* (telephone: 01984 656545).

HAWKRIDGE RESERVOIR AND SPAXTON

❧❀❧

Towards their south-eastern end the Quantock Hills become less spectacular, with lower summits, fewer combes and less moorland vegetation. The views are more intimate and the scenery more sedate. Long winding streams flow through a landscape of rolling farmland, hedgerows and copses. This walk, along fieldside paths and lanes, follows the Cannington Brook from Hawkridge Reservoir, popular with anglers, to Spaxton, a village with a most curious history.

Hawkridge Reservoir was created in 1960 to supply water to nearby Bridgwater, which has expanded since the Second World War into an industrial little town of some local importance. Aisholt, just ½ mile west of the reservoir, is a pretty, unspoilt village with a 14th century church. The poet Sir Henry Newbolt (1862-1938), who wrote such verses as *Drake's Drum* and the much-quoted line '...play up, play up, play the game', used to spend holidays here, staying at the old schoolhouse. Spaxton, which stands a mile east of the reservoir, is an altogether

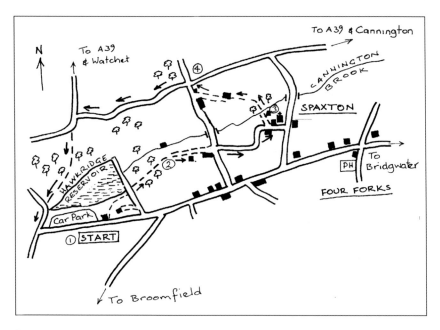

larger, more sprawling settlement. The church here is 15th century (much restored by the Victorians) and there is a rich collection of cottages and farmhouses spread out over a large area, one of the latter (Court House) being a medieval manor house in origin. At the eastern end of Spaxton, in the hamlet of Four Forks, stands the complex of buildings that once housed the infamous 'Agapemone' or the 'Abode of Love'. This was a quasi-religious community founded in 1846 by Henry James Prince, the unfrocked clergyman who had declared himself immortal as the Son of Man. His disciples (many of whom were wealthy and adoring women) called him 'Beloved' and attended to his every wish. He lived in luxurious splendour and took various 'soul brides', at least one of whom bore him a child. Upon Prince's death in 1899 the community found a suitable successor in the Reverend Hugh Smyth Pigott, who continued a lifestyle that local newspapers found difficult to ignore. He died in 1927 but the community surprisingly continued until 1958.

The Lamb Inn stands next to the Agapemone (now sub-divided into private homes). It is a very pleasant, friendly pub selling Ushers ales and a good range of bar snacks and main-course meals, a large blackboard listing daily specials. The main bar room is divided by a large central fireplace and all is dark and cosy with low beamed ceilings

27

and plain walls hung with old farm implements. There are photographs of local scenes and some information about the pub's once-famous neighbours. Normal pub times are kept but the inn closes some weekday lunchtimes. Telephone: 01278 671350.

- **HOW TO GET THERE:** Hawkridge Reservoir is 6 miles north of Taunton and 5 miles west of Bridgwater. It can be reached from the A39, turning south from near Nether Stowey.
- **PARKING:** There is a car park at the side of the reservoir.
- **LENGTH OF THE WALK:** 4 miles. Map: OS Landranger 182 Weston-super-Mare and Bridgwater (GR 205361).

THE WALK

1. From the reservoir car park walk eastwards along the road, keeping the lake to your left. Very soon after passing the house called 'Gatesmoor', on the left, is a stile, also on the left. Climb this and cross the field diagonally down to another stile. On the far side of this you can continue eastwards close to the lake edge, no doubt passing anglers on your way. There is a tarmac track here, serving a wooden clubhouse, and this can be followed. At the far end of the reservoir, beyond the dam and above the water outflow buildings you will find a stile. It is half hidden by the hedgerow to the left of a metal field gate. Cross over this and proceed downhill, diagonally towards the trees at the valley bottom. In the far corner another stile leads on to a most attractive path running through a small woodland. The Cannington Brook flows immediately below, down to the left.

2. In due course you reach a gate, and a bridge over a tributary stream. Beyond these a clear, wide trackway leads straight on. An attractive, but not old, house stands close by, on the riverbank. All in all, this is a most attractive spot. Follow the trackway, as it runs between hedgerows all the way to Spaxton, passing Fishers Farm on the way. At first the track is earthy but later becomes roughly metalled. At the road junction go straight on along Church Road. This bends somewhat but eventually reaches St Margaret's church. The route continues just before this church but time should be allowed to look around this interesting building. The tower dates from 1434 and inside the church are some wonderful 16th century pews.

3. West of the churchyard, from Church Street, follow the No Through

Parking at the side of the reservoir

Road that goes down beside the wall of Peart Hall and ends at Old Mill House. After admiring the garden of the latter and crossing Cannington Brook continue uphill along a grassy track, towards a farm gate. To the right of this gate the path continues, now climbing beneath a line of trees. This 'green lane' is narrow, dark and rather overgrown but very clear since it runs between hedgerows. At the top you leave the trees behind, climbing a stile and proceeding diagonally across a field. Aim for the distant trees where there is a group of barns. Views open out to the left, across the Cannington Valley. On the far side of the field a gate leads you through to a trackway. Follow this towards the houses ahead, where you meet the road.

4. The way back is now very easy, first along some quiet country lanes and then by a bridleway. Turn right along the road to reach a junction and then left in the Aisholt direction. This lane winds around a little for ½ mile and then joins a road, coming up from the right. Keep left here to reach a point where the road bends sharply right. Now go straight on along a wide stony trackway. This runs up to a woodland on the skyline. At the far end of this woodland are two gates. Go through the one on the left and bear right. The reservoir will soon appear down to the left. Continue along the top edge of two fields, keeping the hedgerow to your right. At the far end of the second field the path descends round to the right and continues through a small woodland to a gate and the road. Turn left to reach the reservoir and left again to reach the car park.

PLACES OF INTEREST NEARBY

Fyne Court (3 miles south of Spaxton) is now the headquarters of the Somerset Wildlife Trust and the grounds are open to the public. The National Trust has done a fine job preserving the gardens and creating various woodland walks (telephone: 01823 451587). Closer to Taunton, *Hestercombe Garden* should not be missed. Owned by Somerset County Council this estate is being restored to the designs originally planned by Sir Edwin Lutyens and Gertrude Jekyll (telephone: 01823 337222).

WALK 6

HILLFARRANCE BROOK AND MILVERTON

The Hillfarrance Brook is a tributary of the river Tone. It rises close to the pretty, bustling little town of Wiveliscombe and meanders through a well-timbered landscape to join the Tone just west of Taunton. This walk follows a short stretch of the Brook, east of Milverton – itself a miniature urban gem – and includes a visit to the hamlet of Preston Bowyer and a return by an old railway line and mill race.

The mill race near Milverton

The countryside between the Blackdown Hills, to the south, and Brendon Hills, to the north, is unspoilt and largely unexplored by most visitors to Somerset. It is a hilly area, drained by the river Tone and its tributaries. Since Saxon times the Hillfarrance Brook has played an important part in the economic landscape of this part of Taunton Vale. For almost its entire length it was used to generate power, a long line of watermills developing upon its banks. Indeed the name 'Milverton'

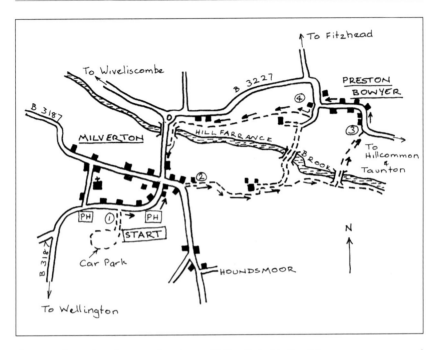

derives from 'settlement by the mill-ford'. Initially this power was used to grind corn but later – by the Middle Ages – it was an essential part of cloth manufacturing. Also by the Middle Ages the Hillfarrance waters were used in both brewing and cider making. Beer is still made at Wiveliscombe, by Exmoor Ales. Watermills remained an important feature of the Hillfarrance valley until the 19th century and today there remains a great selection of scenic additions to the landscape: old mill buildings (many now converted to other uses), mill races, mill ponds and weirs. Several of these are seen on the walk described below.

Milverton dates from the time of the West Saxons but its present appearance results from its growth after the Norman Conquest. The interesting grid pattern of its street layout signifies that it was 'planned' in medieval times, probably as a centre for markets and fairs. Prosperity evidently continued until the 18th century since the town has a wealth of elegant Georgian buildings. North Street, especially, contains some wonderful classical facades. St Michael's church, at the top end of town, dates from the 13th century but is largely Perpendicular in style. Inside are some fine tombs and monuments.

There are two pubs in Milverton, both in Fore Street, the White Hart and the Globe. The latter is a cosy, friendly establishment with two small bar rooms, one of which has a pool table. There are beamed ceilings, plain walls and numerous ornaments hung around, together with photographs of old farming scenes. Good wholesome home cooking is offered with a full selection of bar snacks and main meals. The Sunday lunches are very popular. The real ale served is aptly the local Exmoor brew, from Wiveliscombe. Telephone: 01823 400534.

- **HOW TO GET THERE:** Milverton is 7 miles west of Taunton, beside the B3227 road to Wiveliscombe. Wellington is just 3 miles to the south.
- **PARKING:** There is ample space in the side streets but the free car park down Creedwell Orchard, off Fore Street, is most convenient.
- **LENGTH OF THE WALK:** 2½ miles. Map: OS Landranger 181 Minehead and Brendon Hills (GR 123257).

THE WALK

1. From the public car park walk up to Fore Street and turn right. Continue past The Globe and follow Silver Street round to the left. Turn right along Turnpike, a lane opposite North Street and signposted to Houndsmoor. Where Turnpike bends right, becoming Houndsmoor Lane, go straight on along a wide grassy path. This brings you to the edge of Milverton, where there is a stile and footpath signpost. Follow the direction indicated, straight on across the field.

2. Keeping to the top edge of the field, with a view across the Hillfarrance valley to the left, you will soon reach a small metal gate on the far side, shortly before the hedgerow kinks away to the right (indicating where a former hedgerow must once have stood). Through this gate cut half right diagonally across a small field to another metal gate. Here an arrow disc points the way forward. Continue along the edge of the next very large field, keeping the hedgerow to your left. At the top of a short rise a bench seat has been conveniently positioned, where you can sit and admire the view. The route onward is very clear. Continue along the field edge, to pass alongside a farmstead. Beyond this follow a gravel track to a point where it bends sharply left. There is a sewage works to the left (unseen behind the trees). At the bend go through the gate on the right and continue in the same direction as before, now along another field edge. The Hillfarrance Brook is close at hand, on your left: a pretty, fast-flowing stream bubbling along beneath the trees. Soon you reach a point where you can cross the

The Hillfarrance valley seen from Milverton

Brook. Do so, and then strike up across a large field. Aim to the right of the distant buildings. At the top of the field a gate leads on to the road. Turn left.

3. Walk through the hamlet of Preston Bowyer. There are some handsome buildings here but nothing to indicate the past importance of the place. It was once a wealthy manor held by Goldcliff Priory, Monmouth (12th century) and more recently contained a large silk-throwing factory (19th century). At the western end of the settlement, where the main road turns right, go down the lane to the left, beside a red telephone kiosk. This takes you past some houses and gardens. Soon the lane bends right. Here, on the right, you will see a footpath sign to Milverton. Go through a kissing gate, descend some concrete steps and continue along a very clear, if narrow, footpath.

4. This last stretch should interest the industrial archaeologist. All the way to Milverton the path follows the course of an old railway. Beyond the large building that you soon pass (a converted mill), the path also accompanies an old mill race, along which Hillfarrance waters were diverted in order to turn a waterwheel. With the old rail route, overgrown, to the right and the still-flowing mill race to the left, this is a splendid walk. The path at first runs along below the trees but later, beyond a stile, it follows a wide grassy ride, where the hedgerows are 20 yards apart. This section is clearly the line of the old trackway. In due course, beyond another stile, you pass alongside some back gardens and continue to the road. This can be reached either by way of a flight of steps or else by following the path as it bends left, to join the road close to a timber yard. Milverton is ahead and, perhaps, the pub awaits.

PLACES OF INTEREST NEARBY
At Bradford-on-Tone (4 miles south-east) is *Sheppy's Cider Farm Centre* where there is a rural life museum, cider-making video, tastings and shop, nature walks and a children's play area (telephone: 01823 461233). At Bishops Lydeard (4 miles north-east) is the southern terminal of the *West Somerset Railway* from where steam trains run to Minehead (telephone: 01643 704996).

THE BRIDGWATER AND TAUNTON CANAL AT CREECH ST MICHAEL

The restored Bridgwater and Taunton Canal, together with the meandering lower river Tone, provide pleasant companions for this country stroll from the interesting village of Creech St Michael. Naturally the ground is flat throughout the route, and all the paths are easy to follow, with distant views to the Quantocks and the Brendon Hills.

The canal at Creech St Michael

The river Tone gave its name to the town of Taunton and hence to Taunton Vale, a lush agricultural landscape that has been intensively farmed since Celtic times. To the north of the Vale are the Quantock Hills, to the south the Blackdowns and these grassy uplands dominate all distant views. The Bridgwater and Taunton Canal was opened in 1827. It was intended to be part of an ambitious scheme to link Bristol with Exeter, allowing coal and iron to be brought cheaply to the south coast. But such a plan never materialised and the coming of the railways put an end, in any case, to the age of canals. This particular stretch continued to be used until 1907 but fell into decay thereafter. Restoration took place in the 1980s and 1990s and today the whole length has become something of a tourist attraction. Access has been encouraged with car parks, picnic sites and numerous signposts and provision is made for cycling, fishing and boating. Trips are available on narrow boats.

Creech St Michael, where the walk begins is a large, sprawling village, but a very interesting one. The church, at its southern end, dates back to the 13th century and contains some fine tombs, carvings and memorials. In 1842 the Chard canal opened (linking that town with Ilminster and Taunton) and this joined the Bridgwater and Taunton Canal just to the west of Creech, thus bringing renewed importance and growth to the village. Later in Victorian times the Great Western

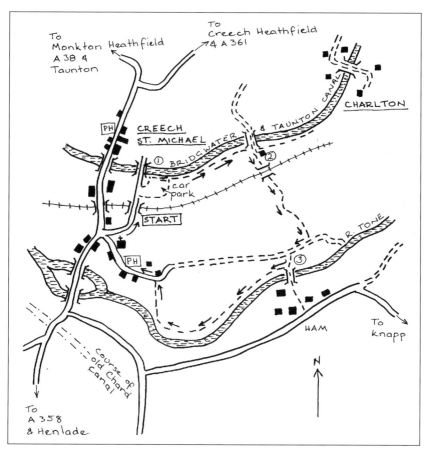

Railway came this way and the Creech Paper Mills were established. Continued expansion was assured.

There are two very good pubs in Creech St Michael. On the main road through the village, north of the canal, is the Bell (telephone: 01823 443703) a freehouse serving a wide selection of food and drink. It is popular, especially in summer when the garden can fill up at weekends. Down Bull Street, close to the church, is the Riverside Tavern. This freehouse serves John Smith and Whitbread ales and boasts an extensive bar snack and main meal menu. The daily specials, written on the blackboard, are usually imaginative and tasty – such as honey and mustard chicken sizzler, Thai chicken with lemon and pepper, and mussels in garlic. This is a large, spacious inn with a high-ceilinged bar room decorated with old photos of the village and country brassware. Telephone: 01823 442257.

- **HOW TO GET THERE:** Creech St Michael is 3 miles east of Taunton, close to the M5 (Junction 25). The village stands between the A38 and A358.
- **PARKING:** Vehicles can be left in the side streets but, preferably, in the large free car park next to the canal at the end of Vicarage Lane.
- **LENGTH OF THE WALK:** 2½ miles. Map: OS Landranger 193 Taunton & Lyme Regis (GR 274255).

THE WALK

1. The Bridgwater and Taunton Canal adjoins the car park, and access can be gained to the towpath through a gate. Walk eastwards along the towpath keeping the canal to your left-hand side. This is a very pleasant stretch and a few bench seats have been positioned to allow for leisurely stops. After about ½ mile you reach a bridge over the canal, this carrying a trackway that runs northward to Creech Heathfield. Those planning alternative walks to the present circuit can follow this trackway, which meanders across open farmland. Otherwise, they may choose to continue along the canal towpath as far as Charlton, a pleasant hamlet set amongst orchards. The circular walk being described here, however, leaves the canal and turns south.

2. Upon reaching the bridge over the canal turn right, crossing a stile next to a gateway which announces 'Private Land'. The land is indeed private but the footpath is public. Keeping to the right of all the buildings that comprise the farmstead, continue along a clear grassy path. This leads to the railway line. Obeying the 'Stop, Look, Listen' sign go through a kissing gate and cross the rail track. On the far side you will see two more kissing gates. Go through the one to the left (displaying an arrow disc) and proceed along a field edge, keeping the hedgerow and stream to your right. In the next corner cross a stile and continue straight on to a second stile. Beyond that one bear half left in the direction indicated by an arrow disc. Walk diagonally across a large meadow to a gate and stile in the far corner amongst a group of trees. Thereafter turn right down a wide earthy track, for about 50 yards and then left over another stile. An arrow disc shows the way: diagonally across a field towards the distant houses. On the far side is a stile that takes you on to the bank of the river Tone.

3. Do not cross the long footbridge, which would take you into the hamlet of Ham. Instead turn right and follow the riverbank. The wide, meandering Tone (on your left) now takes you all the way back to Creech St Michael. But hurry not. It is a fine river and should be appreciated at a leisurely pace. In due course a stile takes you on to a road at the southern end of the village. Turn left for the Riverside Tavern, the church and village centre. If you have time, explore the remains of the old Chard canal.

PLACES OF INTEREST NEARBY

At Hatch Beauchamp (4 miles south-eastwards) is *Hatch Court*, a fine Palladian style mansion surrounded by pretty gardens and a parkland where deer roam. The estate is privately owned but opens to the public on specific days (telephone: 01823 480120). At Stoke St Gregory (5 miles eastward) is the *Willows and Wetlands Visitor Centre*, where there is a museum/exhibition/shop based on basket making and associated crafts (telephone: 01823 490249).

THE BLACKDOWN STREAMS, CORFE AND PITMINSTER

This is a pleasant stroll along and between the little streams – the Broughton and Sherford brooks – that flow down from the Blackdown Hills escarpment. The landscape is one of valleys, meadows and rolling hill country. This walk is from Corfe to the peaceful little village of Pitminster, returning through the ancient Barton Grange estate.

Pitminster

Corfe, where the walk begins, is a pleasant little village which stretches down from the lower slopes of the Blackdowns along the valley of Broughton Brook. There is a scatter of farms and thatched cottages along the main street and the picturesque Norman-style church dates from 1842. Pitminster, just a mile to the west, is the quieter of the two villages. The church here dates from the early 14th century and boasts a fine octagonal tower supporting a leaded spire. A little stream, known as Sherford Brook, trickles behind the cottages mostly unseen by the car-borne traveller. The countryside covered by these two parishes, and traversed by this circular walk, has an interesting history. It once formed part of the manor of Taunton Deane, an estate given by King Athelstan in AD 938 to the Bishops of Winchester. By the Middle Ages there was an important deer park here, supplying venison to the kings of England. In the 16th century, after the Reformation, the state was split up between landowners. The Hill family built Poundisford Lodge and Poundisford Park (both fine mansions sadly not open to the public) and the Colles family built Barton Grange (now mostly demolished). The latter is seen on the walk.

Refreshments can be obtained at both villages. At Pitminster, the Queen's Arms (telephone: 01823 421529) offers a good selection of food and drink in a lovely old-world atmosphere. It is a freehouse

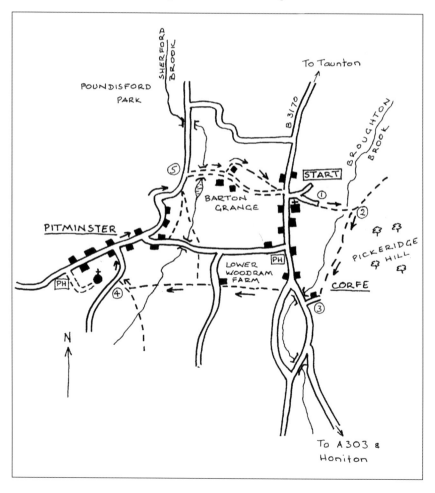

which also has a restaurant and offers accommodation. At Corfe there is the White Hart Inn. This maintains normal pub opening times except for Saturdays when there is all day opening. Inside is a large open-plan bar room with low ceilings, stone walls and a piano. Cotleigh and Flowers beers are served and the food is excellent, from sandwiches and ploughman's lunches to salmon, Cumberland sausages and regular vegetarian dishes. There are menu cards plus daily specials written up on a blackboard. Telephone: 01823 421388.

- **HOW TO GET THERE:** Corfe is just 4 miles south of Taunton, on the B3170 road.
- **PARKING:** Cars can be left, within reason, anywhere in the village but the main road should be avoided if possible. There is parking space close to the church, at the start of the walk.
- **LENGTH OF THE WALK:** 3½ miles. Map: OS Landranger 193 Taunton & Lyme Regis (GR 232197).

The Walk

1. From the church walk eastwards down the lane that runs alongside the graveyard. Where the tarmac surface ends continue straight on, past Old Mill House, to a field gate. Through this the route continues as a grassy path beside a hedgerow. The wooded Pickeridge Hill is now to your right and Corfe village is left behind. On the far side of the kissing gate (which is soon reached) is Broughton Brook, down amongst the trees to the right. The path continues along a field edge until, at the corner, a long, narrow footbridge takes you across the waters of this most attractive little stream. Linger awhile and enjoy the tranquillity of the spot.

2. After crossing the footbridge turn right, following the footpath signposted to Brook Farm. The route is now southwards, with Broughton Brook in its wooded cutting close to your right and the tree-covered hills to your left. A pretty stretch this: through several fields the path crosses a series of hedgerows and there is much wildlife to observe. In due course you reach a pedestrian gate labelled Brook Farm House. Go through this and continue in the same direction. Another gate takes you across a lawn and between some old stone barns to a gravel track. Turn right for the B3170 road. Brook Farm itself is a fine old thatched building, half hidden among the trees on the banks of Broughton Brook. It can best be seen in winter months when the leaves have fallen!

The 19th century church at Corfe

3. Turn right along the B3170 and then, close to the Corfe village sign, left up Adcombe Lane. Beyond the few houses along here, as the lane bends left, there is a gate and footpath signpost on the right. Walk in the direction indicated, east across the meadows, through a number of fields. The path itself is not wonderfully clear but the route is well marked by arrow discs, fixed to all the stiles and gates used. By field edges you soon reach Lower Woodram Farm, just before which you take the left-hand gate (not the gate straight ahead) in order to skirt around the barns. A pedestrian gate then leads you across a farmyard to the road. Go through the gate on the far side and continue in the same direction. More arrow discs, stiles and plank bridges will bring you soon to Pitminster, emerging onto a track close to the church. Turn right.

4. The Queens Arms can be found on the far side of the churchyard, down a lane at the western end of the village. Otherwise the walk continues down the track, right at the junction and straight on at the village centre (following the signs to Poundisford). The road pass a line

43

of houses, winds a little and leaves the village as a pretty tree-shaded lane. Soon you reach footpath finger-signs on the right. Ignore these and walk on another 100 yards. Now take the wide earthy track that leads off to the right at an angle, marked by a large old-fashioned style footpath sign.

5. The way back to Corfe is now both easy and curiously interesting. It leads through the old estate of Barton Grange, once owned by the Bishops of Winchester. The track leads you over an old stone bridge and up to the main house (now converted to flats). Be sure to explore the wooded spot to the right of the stone bridge. Here the Sherford Brook was once dammed, to create a series of fish ponds used in medieval times. The house itself is a mixture of classical and gothic. It is, in fact, the converted old servants' block; the original 16th century mansion has sadly gone. Opposite the back of the house take the footpath signposted through the trees. To give privacy to this group of buildings the public right of way skirts around the old stable block, following the old garden walls, and thence cuts diagonally across a field. Soon you reach the Corfe village hall and, beyond that, Corfe church.

PLACES OF INTEREST NEARBY

On the crest of the Blackdown Hills above Corfe, 4 miles to the southeast is *Castle Neroche*, an Iron Age hill fort and site of an 11th century castle. There are walks through the Forestry Commission woodland and splendid views across Taunton Vale. Another famous local viewpoint is the *Wellington Monument*, 8 miles to the west. This was built in the middle of the 19th century to commemorate the victor of the Battle of Waterloo, who chose the name of the nearby town as the title for his Dukedom.

THE WESTPORT CANAL, HAMBRIDGE AND THE LEVELS

North of Ilminster the Somerset Levels are drained by a number of meandering rivers – the Isle, the Parrett and the Yeo being the largest. It is an area of wide skies, marshy vegetation and an abundance of wildlife. The Westport canal, a half-forgotten waterway, cuts through the middle of this landscape. The following walk traces its entire course from Hambridge to Westport, along the remnants of the old towpath, and you can choose whether to return along a country road or one of the droves that cut across the levels.

The Westport Canal

Throughout the great days of canal building there was the dream, and the engineering challenge, of cutting a waterway from the Bristol Channel to the English Channel. Such a waterway never came about, but stretches of canal were built to link inland Somerset with the docks at Bridgwater. One such was the Westport Canal, which opened in 1840. The aim was to connect the navigable section of the river Isle

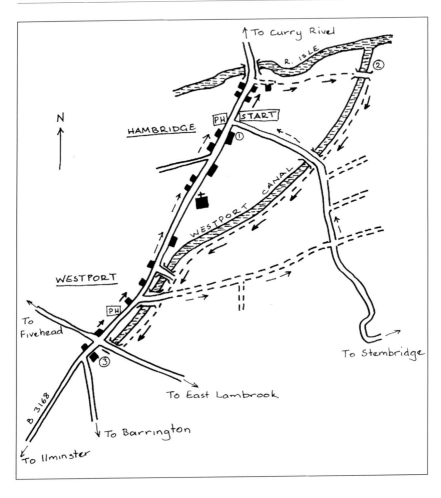

(near Langport) to a place more easily reached overland from such towns as Crewkerne, Beaminster and Bridport. (The last named had a large rope and twine trade and needed a cheap transport link with Bristol.) This new canal proved a great success, but not for long. In 1842 the Chard-Ilminster-Taunton Canal opened, which took away much of its traffic. Within ten years the railways had come to Somerset and the entire canal network had begun its sad decline. By the 1960s the Westport Canal was not only dry but almost lost and forgotten. Today it is in a slightly happier state. Intermittent restoration over the last two decades has brought the water back to the channel and cleared the banks of undergrowth. The towpath is now walkable, as a narrow grassy path through lush marsh vegetation. Westport has some interesting buildings connected with the old canal terminus including a large warehouse, now turned into a very pleasant house. The Old Barn Owl Inn (telephone: 01460 281391) offers a good, old-fashioned welcome with a wide selection of food and drink.

Hambridge, where the walk begins, is a linear village with an interesting variety of buildings. At the southern end is a grand Victorian church. At the northern end is the Lamb and Lion pub where a good range of ales and meals can be obtained. It is an old, attractive building. Inside is a large main bar room and smaller lounge, both with low ceiling beams and plain walls. A large blackboard on the chimney breast lists the daily specials, with such items as sweet and sour chicken, liver and onions, cottage pie and various grills, fish dishes and vegetable bakes. Telephone: 01460 281355.

- **HOW TO GET THERE:** Hambridge stands on the B3168, which links Ilminster with Curry Rivel. It is 10 miles east of Taunton.
- **PARKING:** Cars can be left in any reasonable spot around the village, but preferably not along the B3168 itself. The roads opposite the Lamb and Lion present themselves.
- **LENGTH OF THE WALK:** 5 miles. Map: OS Landranger 193 Taunton and Lyme Regis (GR 395217).

THE WALK

1. From the Lamb and Lion walk north along the B3168, down to the crossing over the river Isle, where stands a pleasant little hamlet. Shortly before the bridge turn right down Water Street, a rather grand name for a short concrete track serving a group of cottages. There is a footpath signpost here pointing to Midelney Bridge. At the end of the track continue in the same direction, through a gate and along a clear earthy path between hedges. Where this stops go through the left-hand gateway (over a little stone bridge) and turn immediately right. In other words, continue in the same direction as before but this time along the edge of a field with a little stream to your right. Soon you reach a bridge. Here is the Westport canal. It joins the river Isle just a short distance to the north from this point. This walk follows its course southwards. Accordingly, cross the bridge and turn right.

2. For nearly 2½ miles you can now enjoy a most pleasant stroll along the canal bank. All the way keep the waterway to your right. There are a few stiles to climb, a few gates to negotiate, a country lane and some tracks to cross but the way is very clear. The path cuts through the meadowbank vegetation and the whole route is a flora and fauna delight. The Somerset Levels stretch out in all directions and the trees along the far side of the canal cast their dappled shade. The route here probably follows the old towpath. The canal itself is water-filled but mostly overgrown by weeds. Here and there you will see the old stone bridges, arched and ivy-covered, which have survived since the canal's heyday. Other bridges are more recent. At the southern end of the canal you can join the B3168 at Westport village. Ignore the first two connecting trackways, and walk until the footpath on the east bank finally ends. This marks the old terminus. Close by, and seen from the village street, are the old warehouses: tall stone buildings now converted to residential use.

3. There is a choice of routes back to Hambridge. The shorter and more direct way is along the B3168. The two villages of Westport and Hambridge almost join and there is a grassy verge most of the way. The road is not busy and there are some interesting old cottages to admire and Hambridge church to explore. The longer and more rural return journey can be made via the droves that cut across the levels – the long straight lanes which dissect the marshes. Follow the drove that runs east from Westport to meet the Hambridge to Stembridge road, then turn left. Both routes fortuitously take you past the Old Barn Owl Inn, so you can fortify yourself before the return journey!

PLACES OF INTEREST NEARBY

Two miles south of Westport is the National Trust property of *Barrington Court*, a Tudor manor house famous for its walled gardens (telephone: 01460 241938). *East Lambrook Manor*, 3 miles eastwards, also has a well-known garden, this being cottage-style created by Margery Fish, the horticulturist and author (telephone: 01460 240328).

THE RIVER PARRETT AT LANGPORT

On the river Parrett, close to its confluence with the river Yeo, stands the little town of Langport, at a gap in the Somerton Hills. To the south are those Levels once dominated by Muchelney Abbey and this walk passes the abbey ruins. They are reached by way of the River Parrett Trail, a long-distance footpath well signposted throughout. The return is by way of the Parrett Cycleway, along the line of an old railway. Both the scenery and wildlife make this a lovely excursion.

Langport was once an important centre for river traffic, the Parrett being navigable this far, but that is not the reason for the place-name's suffix. The 'port' comes from the Saxon word for market place. The town was 'lang' or 'long' because it stretched across a man-made causeway that linked the hills on either side (now occupied by Bow Street). By the 10th century there was a mint here, the place becoming a Saxon royal borough holding regular fairs and markets. In Tudor times a large cloth industry grew up, in due course this spawning a financial sector. Stuckey's Bank was founded in the early 19th century, circulating its own banknotes. The oldest part of town is up the hill, where stands All Saints' church (12th to 16th centuries) and the

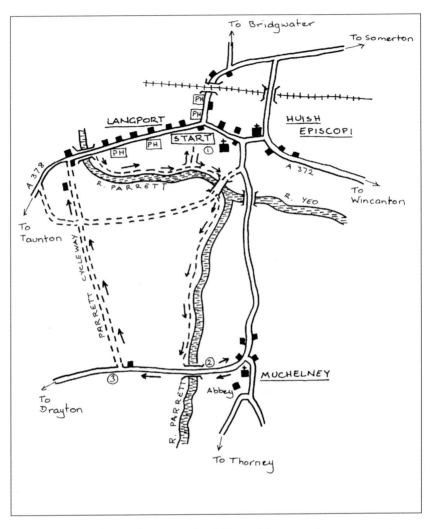

Hanging Chapel, a 15th century building which stands atop an archway across the road. Elsewhere around town there are many old buildings worth a close study above ground level.

Muchelney Abbey was founded in the 17th century and became wealthy on agriculture, draining much of the Levels here. It suffered badly at the Reformation and the ruins are now in the care of English Heritage. In summer months refreshments can be obtained opposite the church at the Stable Tea Room.

No one should go hungry or thirsty in Langport, there being a number of pubs and, along Bow Street, the extremely pleasant Marlborough Tea Rooms. Amongst the pubs the Dolphin Hotel (telephone: 01458 250200) and Old Custom House (telephone: 01458 250332), both in Bow Street, provide the best value food of the plain and wholesome variety. Each is very friendly and truly 'local' in clientele. The Black Swan and the White Lion will be found in North Street.

- **HOW TO GET THERE:** Langport is 13 miles east of Taunton on the A378. It is just 3 miles west of Somerton.
- **PARKING:** There is a large free car park in the centre of Langport, off Cheapside, and it is here the walk begins.
- **LENGTH OF THE WALK:** 4 miles. Map: OS Landranger 193 Taunton & Lyme Regis (GR 420267).

THE WALK

1. At the bottom end of the Langport car park is a grassy picnic area, on the banks of the river Parrett, where benches and tables are set out. From here walk south-eastwards (over a long footbridge) to follow the river upstream. The footpath signpost and River Parrett Trail arrow disc point the way to Huish Bridge. The river should be to your right. Soon you reach the named bridge, which you cross. Now continue along the Parrett Trail, this time with the river to your left, in the direction of Muchelney. The route needs little description. There are a few stiles but the path is very clear as it follows the top of the riverbank, or 'levée', all the way. Simply enjoy the views across the meadowlands. The tower of Muchelney church can be seen ahead and, in the distance beyond, the slopes of Ham Hill. The ridge on the far southern horizon, to your right, is Windwistle Hill.

The Parrett Trail is a 50 mile route following the river from source to mouth, across the entire width of Somerset. It was created through co-operation between various bodies like British Waterways, English Nature, the local councils, country landowners and RSPB. As part of the planning it has been closely connected with education, artistic and craft projects, and many hard working volunteers help maintain access and organise walks, talks and entertainments.

2. Upon reaching the road, turn left for Muchelney Abbey. Only the Abbot's lodging and barns survive but these – together with the excavated foundations of church and cloisters – are well worth visiting. Opposite the present church is the Priest's House, a late medieval hall

Muchelney Abbey

house now owned by the National Trust. Also near the village is Muchelney Pottery, where John Leach produces and sells hand-thrown pots and runs open days.

The walk continues back down the road across the Parrett Trail, over the bridge and on for about 200 yards. There you will see, on the right, an old railway house (still inhabited) and, upon either side of the road, the stone piers of an old railway bridge. Very shortly beyond these, on the right, is the sloping trackway that marks the Parrett Cycleway, a signpost pointing the way to Langport.

3. The route is very straight and very clear. It marks the old Yeovil to Taunton railway line, which ran up through Martock to join the main line from Frome (still in use) a mile west of Langport. South Somerset District Council has done a wonderful job in turning this once overgrown trackway into a most pleasant cycle and walking route. The hedgerows either side are thick and rich in wildlife and the views across the Levels are extensive (since the alignment runs along an embankment). At the far end, where the Cycleway reaches the road at Langport, is the Langport and River Parrett Visitor Centre where information is generously given and walking and cycling equipment can be acquired. The way back to the car park is now either straight along Bow Street or around by the river bank (turning right immediately after the bridge).

PLACES OF INTEREST NEARBY

West of Langport (4 miles) is the *West Sedgemoor Nature Reserve* where hides allow birdwatching across the Levels and into a heronry. At Burrow Hill, west of Kingsbury Episcopi (4 miles south) is *Somerset Cider Brandy Company's Cider Farm* where you can watch, sample and purchase (telephone: 01460 240782).

THE RIVER BRUE AT MEARE

❧❦❧

The Levels north of the Polden Hills, drained by the lower reaches of the river Brue, are dominated by tower-topped, mystical Glastonbury Tor. You will see the Tor in the distance on this walk, which follows a section of the river Brue, and its tributary streams, from Meare, a village with a long and curious history. The footpaths used for the outward journey run along the top of raised riverbanks, or 'levées'.

A bridge over the river Brue

Until the 17th century Meare was an island village. It was cut off from surrounding villages by Meare Pool, a 2-mile wide sheet of water to the north, and by Shapwick Marsh to the south. The inhabitants appear to have lived almost entirely upon fish. In the Middle Ages this area was owned by Glastonbury Abbey and was used for supplying fish to the monks. The Abbots' Fish House, behind the church, is a 14th century survival of that period. Abbey fishermen lived on the first floor and used the ground floor for salting and storing their catch. St Mary's church is largely 15th century and contains some fine medieval wrought-iron work on its south door. On the other side of the road is a handsome Victorian school building, and down Church Path nearby are some pretty cottages. In 1895 a discovery was made, just outside the village, of a much earlier habitation. The remains of two Iron Age 'lake villages' were excavated, showing evidence of a settlement numbering more than 200 stilted huts. It is thought the Celts lived here seasonally, grazing animals in summer and holding regular markets and fairs.

The village inn stands at the western end of Meare. Now called the Countryman but once the 'New Inn', this is a very friendly and popular place. It is large inside, with an open plan bar room, a skittle alley and, at the back, the 'Squires Restaurant'. There are pool and darts facilities and children are welcome. A very wide range of food is offered from bar snacks to multi-course main meals, whilst daily specials are listed on a blackboard. Telephone: 01458 860225. At Westhay, and passed on the walk described below, is the Bird in Hand which is also a pub to be recommended. This dates from 1853 (as announced on the front

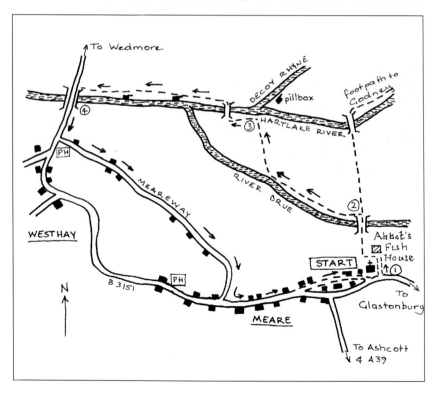

wall) and boasts two bars, a skittle alley, patio garden and a wide range of real ales and home-cooked dishes. Telephone: 01458 860229.

- **HOW TO GET THERE:** Meare is 3 miles west of Glastonbury on the B3151 road to Wedmore. It can also be reached from Ashcott, near Street, by a turning off the A39.
- **PARKING:** Vehicles can be left along the village street where space permits. The Countryman has a very large car park.
- **LENGTH OF THE WALK:** 3½ miles. You will find that some gates must be used as stiles, as not all local farmers conscientiously maintain the public rights of way. Map: OS Landranger 182 Weston-super-Mare & Bridgwater (GR 456417).

THE WALK

1. The walk begins at the church. Walk down the walled pathway that runs between the graveyard and Manor House Farm. Those wishing to view the Abbots' Fish House can obtain the key from the latter. Beyond the gate at the end of the path turn left, to walk behind the church and then right, through a gate, to a long cowshed. Now cross over the fine stone bridge ahead, that takes you across the river Brue. The popular walk across the Levels to Godney starts from this point. Those following the present circuit, however, should turn left immediately after crossing the bridge.

2. The route to Westhay is easy to follow since it runs alongside watercourses the whole way. Follow the Brue riverbank westwards, keeping to the edges of three fields and going through two gateways. Just before the third gateway bear right and cross a stone stile, that takes you across a side ditch. Now follow the edge of a drainage channel along which a line of small trees has grown. Glastonbury Tor should now be seen in the distance to the right. Soon you reach the wide Hartlake river, at a point where it is joined by the Decoy Rhyne. You should see a wartime pill box on the far bank. Turn left.

3. Walk beside the Hartlake river until you reach a bridge. Cross this and continue along the other bank. The waterway should now be on your left. The route is now straight all the way to Westhay. There are more gateways to go through, and two pill boxes to pass, but the route is clear. Half way along you rejoin the river Brue. All around are the spreading meadowlands and you will be unlucky not to see herons.

Manor Farm, Meare

The Wedmore ridge can be seen on the northern skyline. In due course you reach the road. Turn left, over the bridge into Westhay village.

4. At the Bird in Hand pub turn left along Meareway. This runs for a mile all the way back to the western end of Meare. It is a tarmac lane but is pleasant to walk along nonetheless. It is narrow with almost no traffic. Dotted along it are some interesting houses and cottages, whilst the views through the hedgerows either side stretch across the watery landscape. At the far end turn left to return to the church along the B3151, or right to reach the Countryman.

PLACES OF INTEREST NEARBY

Just north of Westhay is *Westhay Moor* where there are bird-watching facilities. To the south of Westhay is the *Peat Moors Visitors Centre* which explains the history of peat digging in this area together with the discovery of local prehistoric causeways called 'Sweet Tracks' (telephone: 01458 860697).

THE RIVER YEO AT ILCHESTER AND YEOVILTON

The Somerset Levels extend as far south as Ilchester. Here the river Yeo, which rises in the uplands of north Dorset, falls almost to sea level. It meanders across a wide, watery plain, Ham Hill to the south and the Somerton Hills to the north. This walk follows some of these meanders, upstream, before visiting Limington village and returning along the Leland Trail. The Yeovilton Royal Naval Air Station is close by, and air traffic gives this walk an added interest.

The river at Northover

Ilchester was once a most important town. It was a major Roman settlement (the Foss Way passing through, dissecting the old road from Dorchester to Street) and the Saxons established both a market and a mint here. From Norman times to the 19th century it was Somerset's county town. In medieval times it boasted a nunnery, a friary and seven churches together with the county gaol and court house. Of all these

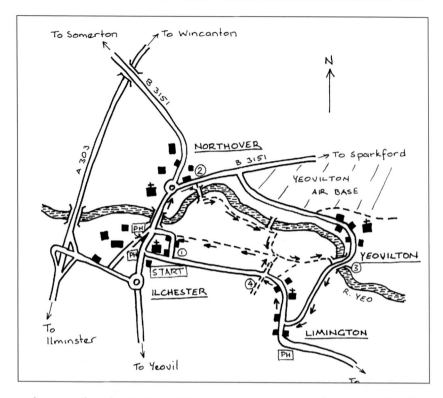

only one church, St Mary Major, survives today. This is mainly 13th century and has an unusually fine tower incorporating Roman bricks and an octagonal top. Elsewhere in the town are some pretty old cottages, a handsome classical Town Hall and a fascinating little museum.

Yeovilton and Limington, villages included in the circular walk, are both worth a visit. The former has a 15th century church, with Norman foundations, and the latter has a selection of very grand houses. One of the rectors at Limington, in the early 16th century, was Thomas Wolsey, who went on to become Henry VIII's powerful Cardinal. North of this stretch of the river Yeo the Naval Air Base dominates the landscape. HMS *Heron* (as it is called) continues to play a major role in Britain's overseas commitments, and the skies above are busy with various planes and helicopters. Indeed, the air traffic gives this particular walk an added interest, especially to those fascinated by aviation.

The Bull at Ilchester is a friendly, unpretentious pub serving a good but simple range of food and drink, including Bass and Butcombe Ales, in a pleasant, no-nonsense atmosphere. The bar rooms are set around a central counter, the ceilings are low and the walls are plain. There is a patio garden at the back. Telephone: 01935 840318.

- **HOW TO GET THERE:** Ilchester is 4 miles north of Yeovil, just off the A303.
- **PARKING:** There is a free car park near the centre of Ilchester, round the corner from the church, in Limington Road.
- **LENGTH OF THE WALK:** 4 miles. Map: OS Landranger 183 Yeovil and Frome (GR 523225).

THE WALK

1. From the town centre walk north along the B3151, crossing the 19th century bridge over the river Yeo. Continue past Northover Manor Hotel (open to non-residents this has a bar, restaurant and children's adventure playground) and bear right at the roundabout. Now adjoined to Ilchester, the village of Northover contains some interesting buildings, including the Old Vicarage, Northover House and the church, which stands high above the road. St Andrew's was largely rebuilt in Victorian times but stands upon an ancient site. Here once stood a Saxon minster church and, before that, a Celtic pagan centre – the hill itself being of prehistoric importance as a religious focal point. Soon after the roundabout you pass alongside the high stone wall of Hainbury Mill Farm, upon the right. At the far end of this is a stile and footpath post. There are two directions indicated. Choose the one pointing to Limington.

2. A clear grassy track, between high hedges, takes you down to a pair of long footbridges, which carry you across the river Yeo. The open meadows now stretch ahead of you (interrupted by lines of flight-path lights since the Yeovilton runway is nearby). The route is clear enough. Follow the riverbank for about ¾ mile, along the edges of several fields and over stiles. In due course you pass a military bridge (private) and bear right, away from the Yeo, to follow a side channel. This leads you to a stone footbridge, which you cross. Continue along the same side channel, over stiles, as it bears left. Soon you reach the far corner of the field where several gateways present themselves. Remember this spot since you will be returning here later in the walk. From this point the way is clear since it becomes a bridleway and follows the Leland Trail. This popular 28 mile long route through South Somerset is

Limington church

regularly signposted with arrow discs. Follow the direction indicated: left to a bridge across a weir and then right alongside a stream to a narrow stone bridge. Continue in the same direction to a gate and then bear left to cross a field diagonally. Soon you reach a gate and a road.

3. Turn left, crossing the bridge over the Yeo, in order to visit Yeovilton, or turn right if you wish to head directly for Limington. It is a very quiet road with little traffic so the walk is very pleasant. Limington village is soon reached, where there is a T-junction. Left will take you to the Lamb and Lark Inn, at the southern end; right will take you to the church at the northern end. The latter direction is also the way of the walk. Beyond the church, after the road has turned left, there is a footpath signpost on the right indicating Yeovilton. Ignore this and walk on another 200 yards. Turn right at the lane marked as a dead-end for traffic, alongside the wall to the large, handsome house called High Barn.

4. Walk down the lane past some attractive old buildings to the far end. Go through the gate straight ahead where there is an arrow disc and bridleway sign. Continue across a bumpy, grassy meadow to the far corner. You should now remember the spot from earlier in the walk. From here you follow the Leland Trail in the opposite direction from before, that is, westwards. Once again the route is clear. Over the stile on the left you follow the direction indicated by the arrow disc. Alongside a hedgerow you continue to another stile, thereafter you head diagonally across a large field down to the bottom corner. There you should find another stile, half hidden in the hedgerow. After this you continue, at first along beside a hedgerow and then across a field. Ilchester is now seen in the distance, directly ahead. There are several more stiles to cross, together with a farm track and a plank bridge but the route is clear all the way to the eastern edge of town.

PLACES OF INTEREST NEARBY

Yeovilton Air Station contains the *Fleet Air Arm Museum*, an extremely popular local attraction. This has an extensive display of historic aircraft, from the earliest flying machines to Concorde 002 (telephone: 01935 840565). South of Ilchester are two well-known National Trust properties: *Tintinhull Garden*, with formal landscaping inspired by Gertrude Jekyll (telephone: 01935 822545), and *Montacute House*, an Elizabethan mansion with magnificent state rooms and regular exhibitions (telephone: 01935 823289).

THE KING'S SEDGEMOOR DRAIN
AND BAWDRIP

This walk follows a section of the King's Sedgemoor Drain, near the village of Bawdrip, one of a number of pretty villages that stretch out along the Polden Hills. The Levels hereabouts give some lovely open views. The paths used are very clear and the entire route is on level ground. There are some stiles to climb, however.

The present appearance of the Somerset Levels is largely man-made. This whole area, from the coast to the hills around Somerton, Wells and Ilminster, was once a vast expanse of marshland. Drainage took place from the 12th century onwards, financed at first by the abbeys of Glastonbury, Muchelney and Athelney but later by a succession of landowners with Government approval. In the 18th and 19th centuries large straight drainage channels were added to the network of smaller 'rhines' and major pumping systems were developed. The King's Sedgemoor Drain was one of these channels.

From the town of Street to the coast north of Bridgwater is a fingerlike ridge that rises above the Levels. This is made of a rock called lias, which is naturally harder than the surrounding alluvial deposits, and is called the Polden Hills. Along these hills are villages which were built above the flood-plain. Many pleasant walks can be enjoyed between and around these pretty, unspoilt little settlements and lovely views can be gained across the broad expanse of the Levels in all directions. The Mendips, Ham Hill, the Blackdowns, Quantocks and often Wales, too, can be seen on the skyline all around. Bawdrip stands at the western end of the Polden Hills, overlooking the point where the King's Sedgemoor Drain cuts through the landscape to meet the river Parrett. The prettiest part of the village is set around the 13th century church, the interior of which should be seen if time permits. There are numerous carved heads, memorials and an interesting staircase in the west tower. The nearby estate belongs to Knowle Hall, a 19th century building now occupied by the British Institute for Brain Damaged Children.

On the main road is the Knowle Inn. This large friendly establishment offers a variety of services: accommodation, a family room, morning coffee, a wide selection of guest real ales and a full range of food. There are regular menu cards (together with a special 'kids' choice) and daily specials are written up on a blackboard. There is everything from sandwiches to salads, fish and vegetarian dishes to grills and steaks. The atmosphere is pleasantly traditional with a large main bar room, a lot of bare wood and plain walls hung with prints and old photographs. Telephone: 01278 683330.

- **HOW TO GET THERE:** Bawdrip is 4 miles north-east of Bridgwater, on the A39. It is 2 miles from Junction 23 on the M5.
- **PARKING:** There is ample parking space in the village down by the church. The Knowle Inn also has a large car park.
- **LENGTH OF THE WALK:** 2½ miles. Map: OS Landranger 182 Weston-super-Mare & Bridgwater (GR 342396).

THE WALK

1. From the church walk southwards down the lane to the edge of the village and continue along Bradney Lane. It is not long before you reach King's Sedgemoor Drain. Cross the bridge and turn right along a gravel trackway that runs through 'Fisherman's Car Park'. There are usually some cars parked here for – as the name suggests – this stretch of waterway is popular with anglers.

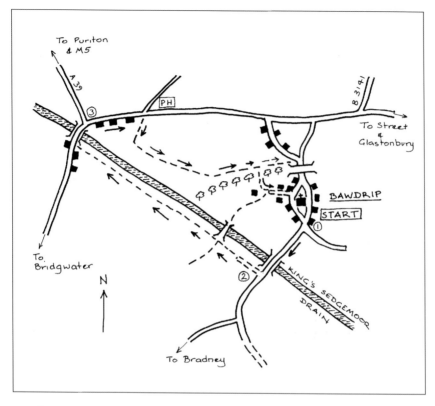

2. The route beside the Drain needs little description. Beyond the first gate and stile the trackway is replaced by a footpath and this is not always very clear. However, you can scarcely go wrong! Continue across a number of fields and through several gateways (or over several stiles) keeping the water course close at hand all the way. To the right, across the Drain, the landscape rises to a line of buildings, which form the top end of Bawdrip. To the left the view is towards Bridgwater, across the wide sweep of meadowland. It is a pleasant stretch and the Drain forms a majestic sheet of water. In due course you reach the road. Turn right, back across the Drain by bridge, and right again at the junction in the Street direction.

3. There is a pavement alongside the A39 and the route takes you past a number of houses and bungalows. At the end of these, almost opposite the Knowle Inn, you will see a public bridleway signpost, pointing to the right. Follow the direction indicated, along a narrow

The Knowl Inn

track that runs between a field and a small industrial site. Soon this track bears left and narrows to a path. The route is very clear, however, as it runs across open farmland. At first, there is a hedgerow either side, later the path accompanies a narrow drainage ditch. In due course, on the right-hand side you walk alongside a belt of trees. This marks the line of an old railway. Here a choice presents itself. Either continue straight on, to reach the old part of Bawdrip village, or turn right where a footpath sign indicates an alternative. The latter route takes you, by flights of steps, across the old railway embankment and then left along a gravel trackway. This will bring you out opposite Bawdrip church.

PLACES OF INTEREST NEARBY

At Westonzoyland (3 miles south) is an interesting *Pumping Station Museum* which is open intermittently to steam enthusiasts and run by volunteers (telephone: 01823 275795). At East Huntspill (3 miles north) is the *Secret World Wildlife Centre*, with a small but interesting collection of native and exotic animals (telephone: 01278 78325).

UPHILL AND THE AXE ESTUARY

*The river Axe rises in the Mendip Hills near Wells and meanders through
the Levels below Cheddar to reach the sea at Brean Down. Parts of its
course have been straightened and canalised over the years but it is still
an attractive waterway. This walk accompanies the river as it emerges
into Weston Bay, around the village of Uphill. The route runs through a
nature reserve and across a saltmarsh to a sandy beach. There are some
lovely coastal views to enjoy and the paths are clear throughout.*

Looking over the bay from Uphill

Before the Somerset Levels were drained, the Axe estuary was a wide
sheet of water stretching from Bleadon Hill to Brent Knoll, which are
3 miles apart. It provided the main access into Somerset for ocean-
going vessels. It is said the Phoenicians sailed up this way when trading
their cloths and jewellery in exchange for English minerals like iron
ore. The Romans also came here and founded a port where Uphill
marina now stands. According to legend, Joseph of Arimathea landed
hereabouts from Palestine, on his way to Glastonbury. Today Uphill is

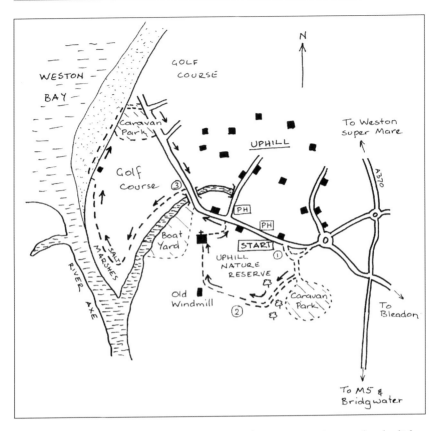

a quiet little town notwithstanding its close proximity to the holiday resort of Weston-super-Mare. The hilltop above the old centre is dominated by two towers, both visited on the walk described below. One is the base of an old windmill, the other is the tower of the semi-ruined Norman church of St Nicholas. Much of this hilltop is also a nature reserve, home for a varied collection of flora and fauna. Along the seafront is a golf course, which backs onto the sand dunes, and offshore is often an interesting profusion of yachts and other small craft since the town has a thriving sailing community.

Along the road below St Nicholas' church (Uphill Way) stands the Old Hall Restaurant and Tea Room together with two pleasant pubs, the Dolphin and the Ship Inn. The Ship calls itself 'the oldest pub in Weston' although the building does not, in truth, suggest great antiquity. It is a very friendly place, however, and very popular with both locals and walkers. The main bar room, on different levels, has a lot of bare woodwork and stone walls, these decorated in keeping with the pub's name. There is also a skittle alley and restaurant. Tetley and Marston ales are served, together with a good range of food from sandwiches upwards. Daily specials are written up on a blackboard and dishes tend to be of the wholesome-and-large portion variety: stews, curries, grills and so on. Telephone: 01934 621470.

- **HOW TO GET THERE:** Uphill is just off the A370 road 2 miles south of the centre of Weston-super-Mare.
- **PARKING:** Vehicles can be left anywhere along the streets of Uphill provided no obstruction is caused. There is a large lay-by at the southern end, near Folly Lane, where the walk begins.
- **LENGTH OF THE WALK:** 2½ miles. Map: OS Landranger 182 Weston-super-Mare & Bridgwater (GR 320584).

THE WALK

1. The walk begins at the eastern end of Uphill Way. From either of the two pubs mentioned above turn left. From the lay-by, where the road bends to join a roundabout, follow the gravel track that leads up past Uphill Caravan Park. Continue through the gate labelled 'Uphill Nature Reserve' along the track ascending through a small woodland. This is, in fact, called Folly Lane. There is an information board here describing

The remains of the windmill at Uphill

the geology and natural history of the area. This is a designated area of special scientific interest and thus should be explored with due consideration. This hilly outcrop is made of limestone and for many years, from the early 19th century to the 1940s, it was the scene of much quarrying. An old lime kiln remains, down by the water's edge and there are some caves beneath the cliffline. Follow the track as it bends right, out of the trees and onto the hilltop.

2. This grassy summit has a most wonderful prospect. The Axe estuary is below, flowing out into the sea. Beyond is Brean Down and, out to sea, the twin islands of Steep Holm and Flat Holm. Wales can be seen on any reasonably clear day. To the north, of course, is Weston-super-Mare. The old windmill, now a stump of a tower, can be climbed by a spiral staircase. Around its viewing platform are panorama boards, identifying the distant points of the skyline: Exmoor, the Quantocks, Mendips and so on round the compass points. From the windmill, cross over to St Nicholas' church and explore this fine building. The descent is from the other side of the graveyard, down a steep grassy path to the road (Uphill Way again). The Dolphin stands nearby. Turn left and walk along the road, as it bends right past the boat yard entrance. Very soon after this bend, turn left, over a stile and along a concrete path.

3. The River Axe should now be to your immediate left-hand side. Soon the path becomes an earth and grass way along the top of a raised river bank or 'levée'. The route is clear as it winds alongside the river and across the salt marshes. Leaving the moored boats behind you eventually arrive at the river's mouth. Here the path seems to disappear into the marram grasses of the sand dunes. Close by, and standing upon stilts, is the wooden Weston Bay Yacht Club building. From here you continue along the coast. There is a path on the top of a sea wall here but the right-of-way actually runs along the back of the beach alongside this wall. At the far end you emerge onto a small caravan site. Through this you continue to a gate from where you turn right. Links Road now takes you back to Uphill Way and your starting point.

PLACES OF INTEREST NEARBY
Weston-super-Mare, of course, has numerous attractions including *Sea Life*, and, inland a little towards Puxton, *The Helicopter Museum* (telephone: 01934 635227).

WALK 15

CHEDDAR RESERVOIR AND AXBRIDGE

This is the edge of Mendip country. On the uplands are such famous beauty spots as Cheddar Gorge and Caves, Ebbor Gorge and Wookey Hole. On the lowlands below are the Axe meadows and Levels around Wedmore, a bird-watchers' paradise. This walk follows the edge of Cheddar Reservoir, a lovely spot popular with fishermen, and then the course of an old railway line – giving views both across the meadows and up to the hills. The paths used are clear, level and dry in all weathers.

The path alongside Cheddar Reservoir

Along the southern edge of the Mendip Hills runs a line of little towns and villages, including Axbridge and Cheddar. Each of these would make a very good centre for walking and touring. Now that Axbridge has been by-passed by the main road it is a quiet, pretty place that centres on a handsome square. This, together with High Street and West Street, is lined by rows of old buildings dating from the 15th to 19th

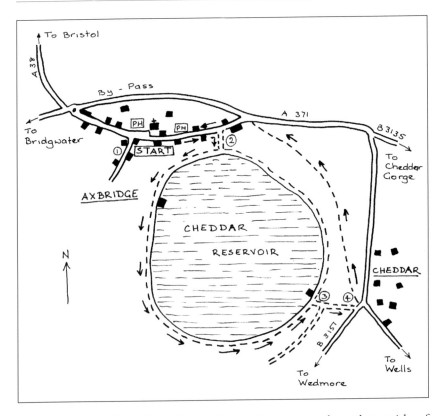

centuries. The tall, timbered King John's Hunting Lodge takes pride of place. This dates from Elizabethan times and was once an inn called the King's Head. It has no known connection with King John although the whole manor here was once a royal estate, at the time of that monarch. Today the building is owned by the National Trust and houses an interesting little museum. Those with time should visit the church at the top corner of the Square. This dates from the 15th century and contains some fine fan vaulting and a plaster ceiling with pendants. The walk described below almost reaches the little town of Cheddar and those with sufficient energy and interest could detour for a closer look. It is larger, busier and more 'touristy' than Axbridge, but still repays a visit. Amongst the old cottages and shops is an old market cross, a 14th century church and the remains of a medieval chapel.

In the main square at Axbridge are the handsome Oak House Hotel and the Lamb Inn, both establishments being recommended to supply a full range of refreshments. The Lamb Inn is a large, traditional establishment with low beamed ceilings, bare stone walls and inglenook fireplaces. There is a main bar room plus several other sitting areas leading off at different levels. Real ales (such as Butcombe), farm cider and a wide selection of food are on offer. There are regular items, and daily specials listed on blackboards, these tending towards the wholesome English variety. The home-made soups are especially good. Telephone: 01934 732253.

- **HOW TO GET THERE:** Axbridge is 9 miles south-east of Weston-super-Mare and 10 miles north-west of Wells. It stands on the A371.
- **PARKING:** There are public car parks in Axbridge, signposted from the town square. Parking is also possible at Cheddar Reservoir.
- **LENGTH OF THE WALK:** 4½ miles. Map: OS Landranger 182 Weston-super-Mare & Bridgwater (GR 431546).

THE WALK

1. From the town square walk eastwards along St Mary's Street, past the Crown Inn, a pub especially popular amongst locals. This road soon becomes Jubilee Road and then Cheddar Road, as it heads for the edge of town. There is a pavement all the way. Just before the end-of-speed-limit sign there is a footpath signpost pointing down a tree-lined drive on the right. Follow this, past the signboards proclaiming the Bristol Corinthian Yacht Club and Bristol Water. This drive leads straight to Cheddar Reservoir.

2. This walking route suggests you follow the reservoir's edge anticlockwise. Those who wish to shorten the total length of their excursion can, of course, go clockwise. Either way, it is a very pleasant stroll, and indeed, very popular. The pathway is firm and gravelled, thus being walkable even during the wettest periods of our unpredictable climate. This sheet of water is well-known amongst anglers as well as walkers and dog owners, so you will probably not be alone on your circumnavigation. You leave the reservoir on the far side close to the pumping station that stands on the south-eastern edge. But do not rush. It is a most pleasant stroll, with views across the meadows southwards towards Wedmore, and up to the Mendips northwards. It is easy to identify the beginning of Cheddar Gorge – a deeply cut valley running up from behind the rooftops of Cheddar village. The aerial mast above Axbridge stands on Fry's Hill.

3. By way of a gateway and stile, and a kissing gate next to a car park, you leave the reservoir along another tree-lined drive. This leads directly to Cheddar. Those wishing to visit this town must cross the busy A371 road. Otherwise, the way back begins immediately before the drive meets the B3151. On the left, across a gravelled parking area, is a sign forbidding horses and motorcycles. This marks the beginning of the cycling and walking path that has been created along the course of an old railway line. Turn left, away from the old railway bridge that carries the B3151.

4. At first this pathway runs along the old railway cutting, with hedgerows either side. Soon, however, it cuts across more open country, but the ground underneath is firm all the way. This alignment was once part of the old Cheddar Valley Railway which linked Wells with the main line at Yatton, beyond the Mendips. To the south of this little stretch the line has disappeared under housing and farming. To the north it provided the route for the Axbridge by-pass. But here the line thankfully provides a pleasant walking route. The local volunteers who established and continue to maintain it should be commended. At the far end you join the main road. Turn left and walk down Cheddar Road, retracing your earlier steps back to Axbridge.

PLACES OF INTEREST NEARBY
Just a short way up from Cheddar is the famous *Gorge* and its associated networks of caves. Here there is interest for all the family: guided walks are conducted underground and courses are run for climbing, caving and abseiling. There are also numerous shops and craft centres to visit. Telephone: 01934 742343.

THE RIVER CHEW AND CHEW MAGNA

The river Chew rises near the village of Chewton Mendip, on the high Mendip plateau, and meanders down, eventually to join the Avon in the Bristol outskirts. This lovely river-side walk, from the pretty village of Chew Magna, explores the Chew Valley as it emerges from the Chew Valley Lake, a large reservoir created in 1956. The route visits Chew Stoke, another attractive village, before returning on field paths across several stiles.

From the northern edge of the Mendips a line of springs issues forth from the limestone escarpment, creating a number of attractive streams, including the river Chew. These flow north to the Bristol Channel, through pleasant undulating, well timbered countryside. Chew Magna is a bustling place with a wonderful mixture of building styles, from old medieval cottages to grand Georgian residences. In Tudor times there was an important cloth industry here, woollens being made, and transported via Bristol to Europe and beyond. The village was also a main centre for markets and fairs, a maypole stood

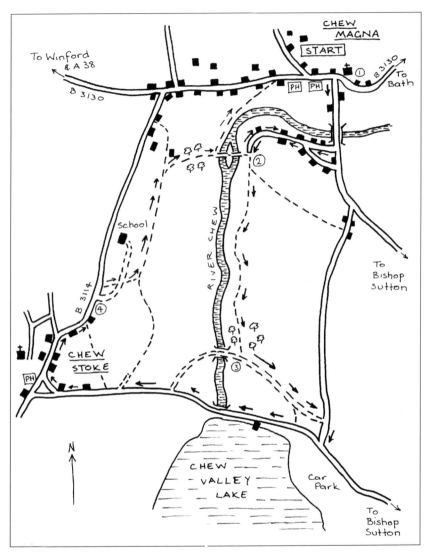

in the High Street until the 18th century and many a rich Bristol merchant moved here rather than mix with the stilted aristocracy at Bath. The tall, handsome church dates back to Norman times and is noted for its stone gargoyles outside and its wooden carvings inside. Nearby is the 16th century Church Ale House, originally used for ecclesiastical festival days but later turned into a school.

Chew Valley Lake, owned by Bristol Water, does not have a public footpath all around its edge. However, there are several access points, with car parks and picnic areas, and some nature trails have been designed allowing walkers to enjoy the varied wildlife along the shoreline. There are public conveniences and a tea shop along the road to Bishop Sutton and a special trackway has been designed to enable the use of wheelchairs. Permits are also available for fishing and bird watching.

Chew Magna has three good pubs and there is a tea shop in the village centre. The Pelican Inn is 18th century and is especially well-known for its menus. These range from toasted sandwiches and rolls to salads, omelettes, curries and steaks. Emphasis is made of wholesome and traditional recipes (such as cottage pie and meat puddings), large portions and reasonable prices. There is also a children's menu. The atmosphere is friendly and the decor is unpretentious with simple furnishings, plain walls and old photographs. Telephone: 01275 332448.

- **HOW TO GET THERE:** Chew Magna is 7 miles south of Bristol, on the B3130 road which links the A38 and A37. It can also be reached from the south, turning off the A368 at West Harptree.
- **PARKING:** There is a free car park behind the Pelican Inn. Vehicles can also be left in the side streets, provided no obstruction is caused.
- **LENGTH OF THE WALK:** 4½ miles. Map: OS Landranger 182 Weston-super-Mare & Bridgwater (GR 576632).

THE WALK

1. From the Pelican Inn walk south down the road signposted to Bishop Sutton and Bath. Cross over the old stone bridge and turn right down Dumpers Lane, which is before the fire station. Incidentally, take a look at the bridge as you cross over. It is 15th century, triple-arched and contains a curiosity. Over the eastern side is a stone trough. This was once used in time of plague, when the village was effectively cut off. Local farmers used to bring food to this spot and collect their payment from the trough, where coins were thrown into sterilising vinegar. Continue all the way to the end of Dumpers Lane which curves left past the handsome Dumpers House. Two signposts greet you: a public bridleway goes to the right (over a wooden footbridge) and a footpath goes straight on, bearing left. Take the latter. You will be returning along the former later on.

2. In fact, very soon the footpath you have chosen divides at a fork, immediately beyond a stile. To the left is a route that cuts across the field towards the buildings on the skyline. Ignore this. Instead follow the route to the right. This follows the edge of the field. The river and its accompanying trees should be close on your right-hand side. From here route-finding is very easy. Cross a number of fields and climb several stiles. Regular arrow discs point the way up the valley and you keep alongside the meandering river Chew most of the way. This is a very pleasant walk and time can be spent looking around. Towards the top you walk through a small woodland and over a wooden footbridge. Thereafter you join a tarmac drive. The bridge on your right is private (Bristol Water property). Turn left along the drive away from this bridge.

3. After a short ascent you reach a gate and stile onto a road. Turn right and then right again at the junction. You now cross the dam that holds the reservoir and the broad expanse of Chew Valley Lake stretches away from you. It is an impressive sight. Continue along the road all the way to Chew Stoke. There is a footpath on the right, signposted down a track that you could take, but this would cause you to miss the pleasant little village, where stands the Stoke Inn. This large country tavern is very popular and offers a good range of both refreshments and facilities. At the junction near this pub turn right along the B3114. Those with time might like to look round that part of the settlement, around the church, which is to the west of this road.

4. The final stretch, back to Chew Magna, begins at the northern edge of the village. Leave the B3114 at the Chew Valley Rugby Football Club. There is a footpath signpost on the right, pointing across the pitches. Follow the direction indicated (or else politely walk around the touch-lines) to the far corner. There you join a track running between hedgerows. Turn left along this for 50 yards and then climb the stile you see on the right-hand side. Walk across the field diagonally towards the trees in the valley ahead. Cross the stile in the far corner and continue in the direction shown by an arrow disc. The route is now almost dead straight, across a number of fields and stiles. Arrow discs show the way, along the side of the Chew valley. Keep the school buildings to your left and the view across the river to your right. At one point you enter the school grounds and must walk around the top end of a playing field before resuming the same direction.

Chew Valley Lake

In due course you will see Chew Magna ahead and some large detached houses up to your left. Do not climb the stile in the top corner, by a farmstead. Instead cross the stile along the hedgerow and bear right downhill across a large field. Beyond another stile follow a clear path, descending beneath a belt of trees. From here you will soon see a stile on the right-hand embankment. Cross this, walk down a field edge to the bottom corner and then climb the last stile of the circuit. Walk over a most attractive stone bridge, which carries a clear track over the Chew river which divides and widens into a pretty pool here. The next footbridge brings you to the end of Dumpers Lane, from where you can retrace your earlier steps.

PLACES OF INTEREST NEARBY
Just 1½ miles east of Chew Magna is *Stanton Drew Stone Circle*, a Neolithic site which could be 5,000 years old. It was possibly constructed for religious purposes. At Chewton Mendip (7 miles south) is the *Chewton Cheese Dairy*. Here cheese making is demonstrated and produce is sold. There are also a restaurant, shop, picnic area and a collection of birds of prey (telephone: 01761 241666).

THE UPPER MELLS RIVER FROM HOLCOMBE

Few streams flow across the Mendips and the Mells River is the largest. This walk from Holcombe follows part of its upper course, through a fascinating district of past human activity from mining to the canal that never was, with an optional detour to St Dunstan's Well. The paths are clear and the views good, and the walk will also appeal to amateur historians and archaeologists.

The 'lost' Somerset and Dorset Canal passed on the walk

The Mendip Hills are largely made of carboniferous limestone. This has not only led to the general appearance of the countryside with its high, bleak hilltops and numerous caves and gorges (as at Wookey Hole and Cheddar) but also created a distinctive human landscape. From Celtic times onwards minerals have been mined here; lead and silver in earlier times, coal in more recent history and still today stone quarrying continues. Holcombe, like its immediate neighbour Coleford, grew as a coalmining village and most of its buildings date from the Industrial Revolution onwards. It is an interesting place rather than a pretty one – although its location is certainly attractive. It is a long narrow settlement stretching down a hill slope and thus boasts wide views across the surrounding hills. The one spot which is picturesque can be found nearly a mile north of the present village centre, where stands the old parish church. This dates from the 15th century and stands alone amongst farmland. Here lie buried members of the Scott family – for Holcombe was the place where Captain Robert Falcon Scott, the Polar explorer, was brought up. His father was manager of a local brewery. The medieval village of Holcombe, which once stood around the church, disappeared partly because of the Black Death and partly because of the development of the coal mine further down the slope.

At the bottom end of the present village is the area known as Edford, where the road crosses the Mells River. This is where the walk begins and here too stands the Duke of Cumberland Inn. A most pleasant and friendly establishment, this serves several real ales (Butcombe and Flowers, for example) and excellent bar snacks (of the simple and wholesome variety). There is a large bar room with wood panelling and soft bench seats, a function room and skittle alley. Outside is a small, attractive beer garden on the Mells riverbank. Telephone: 01761 232412.

- **HOW TO GET THERE:** Holcombe stands 3 miles south of Midsomer Norton and 5 miles north-east of Shepton Mallet. It is east of the A367 near Stratton-on-the-Foss.
- **PARKING:** Vehicles can be left at any reasonable spot in Holcombe, provided no obstruction is caused. There is a large car park opposite the Duke of Cumberland and the landlord is more than happy to allow patrons to leave their vehicles there.
- **LENGTH OF THE WALK:** 2½ miles. Map: OS Landranger 183 Yeovil & Frome (GR 670488).

THE WALK

1. The footpath begins opposite the Duke of Cumberland, next to the car parking area. The signpost points to Barlake and the route is a clear earthy track running between hedgerows and beneath the trees. However, you do not stay on this track for long, perhaps 100 yards. A stile either side suggests a footpath crossing. Climb the one to the left and go down into a field. Before walking onward look about you. The

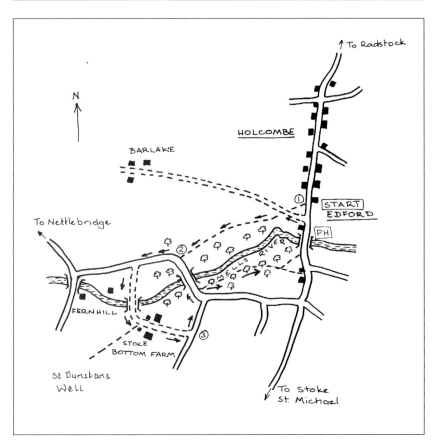

track you were on crossed an old stone arched bridge and, from the field you have climbed down upon, you can see much better its structure. It was built to span a canal that was never finished. The Somerset and Dorset Canal was planned in the late 18th century but only 13 miles of it was ever built. It was meant to go from Nettlebridge to Frome along the Mells valley and then both north to the Avon at Bath and south to the Stow north of Christchurch. But only the stretch to Mells was ever dug and none of it was ever fully used.

From the stile follow the top edge of the field, parallel to the Mells river over to your left. In the far corner go through a gateway and continue along the top edge of a woodland. The humpy ground to the right is evidence of past mining. Over another stile you keep to the woodland edge all the way as it bears left into the bottom corner. There a gate and stile take you onto the road. Turn right.

2. After a few hundred yards the road emerges from the cover of the surrounding trees. To the left is a rough-metalled lane signposted to Stoke Bottom Farm. Follow this since it is a bridleway and hence a public right of way. After crossing the bridge over the Mells River, this lane swings left towards the farm buildings.

For those with time and interest a detour is now an optional extra. The landscape to the west (right) is fascinating to explore, and a footpath that leads into the area begins at a pedestrian gate (opposite the cow shed) on the right before the farmhouse. A short way along, under the steep hill slope in the second field, is the site of St Dunstan's Well next to a pair of stone gate piers. This was once an important source of water: a row of cottages and paper mill stood here. To the north of this spot, in the area on the map named Fernhill, once stood a Georgian mansion called Stoke House. This stood amongst gardens and parkland, the remains of which can be seen all around. The waters from St Dunstan's Well ran through these grounds as waterfalls and rills. The house was demolished before the Second World War. The land is still private.

Continuing the main walk, the lane to Stoke Bottom Farm continues between the buildings, bears left and climbs as a rough stony track to the road. Turn left when you get there.

3. The way back to Holcombe is now straightforward. Continue down the road and turn left at the junction, descending back to the Mells River. Before the bridge, take the footpath on the right. The route now follows the path through Edford Wood Reserve, a lovely stretch. At the far end of the trees cross the field to join the road, either at a small industrial site or else further downhill towards Holcombe. Turn left upon reaching the road.

PLACES OF INTEREST NEARBY

At Cranmore, 4 miles south of Holcombe, is the *East Somerset Railway* where steam train excursions can be enjoyed and an art gallery can be visited (the centre having been founded by artist and conservationist David Shepherd) (telephone: 01749 880417). Of course, the town of *Wells*, 8 miles west, should not be missed, with its cathedral, moated Bishop's Palace and wonderful collection of old buildings and lanes.

THE LOWER MELLS RIVER AT MELLS

As the Mells river descends towards Frome, its valley becomes gorge-like, creating a more spectacular countryside than is found in the stream's earlier stretches. This walk from one of the most attractive villages in the Mendips follows the riverbank along the bottom of a deep, wooded cutting. Here and there are remains of the working past, and the walk returns by Tedbury Camp, an Iron Age hill fort, adding extra interest to a stroll rich in flora and fauna. The route is very clear throughout.

Great Elm visited on the walk

Mells is scattered over a fairly large area, around a network of lanes, and has some wonderfully old buildings. The church largely dates from the 15th century and contains numerous interesting monuments and carvings. New Street, which leads up to the church and is contemporary with it, was designed by Abbot Selwood who intended it to be part of an overall town plan shaped as a cross. The other streets forming that shape were never built. West of the church is Mells Manor (private) dating originally from Tudor times. The gate piers at the

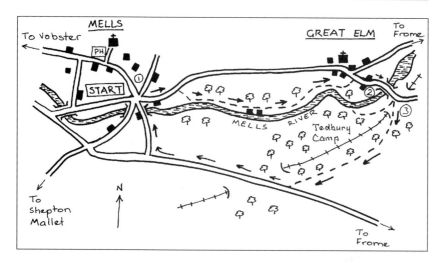

entrance gates are more recent, designed by Edwin Lutyens (as was the village War Memorial). Other buildings of note include a Georgian rectory, a medieval tithe barn and a curious little lock up or Blind House.

The Talbot Inn stands on the corner of New Street. This goes back, in part, to the late 15th century and is a well-known local hostelry. It is deservedly popular since the food offered is excellent and has won numerous awards and medals. The entrance doors are reached through a stone-floored courtyard where tables and chairs are laid out, in the shadow of the nearby church tower. Inside all is dark and cosy with low ceilings and settle seats, bare floors and wooden dado walls. Telephone: 01373 812254.

- **HOW TO GET THERE:** Mells is 3 miles west of Frome, from which it is most easily reached.
- **PARKING:** Vehicles can be left anywhere in the village where space allows and provided no obstruction is caused. Woodlands End, at the eastern end of the village, where six roads meet, is possibly the best place to park for this walk.
- **LENGTH OF THE WALK:** 4 miles. Map: OS Landranger 183 Yeovil & Frome (GR 731490).

THE WALK

1. From Woodlands End, where stands the Mells post office, follow the road eastwards which is signposted Great Elm and Frome. After the

The entrance to Mells Manor

end-of-speed-limit sign this road bends to the left. At this point a gate will be seen on the right, with a bridleway signpost. Follow the route indicated: a clear, firm trackway running beneath the trees. The Mells river is immediately to your right. The way needs little description. The bridleway winds through the trees, along the north bank of the stream, all the way to Great Elm. It is a lovely walk and should not be rushed. Not far along, from the Mells end, the pathway divides as it reaches some old stone ruins. The left-hand route skirts above these ruins, alongside a high wall, and is the one to choose for Great Elm. The right-hand route wanders around the old buildings and becomes lost amongst the stonework. Choose this if you wish to investigate the site. How fascinating it all looks! There are several structures here: warehouse, mill, cottages, perhaps together with the remnants of their gardens. All the roofs have gone, many floors and windows also, and everything is overgrown. A many-arched viaduct can be seen and a long flight of steps. Mells was once an industrial village with water mills, breweries, iron foundries and, for the cloth business, fulling mills. These ruins remind us of this past.

Towards Great Elm, as the valley deepens, the bridleway passes close to a house, which is served by a roughly metalled access road.

Do not walk along this uphill. Instead keep to the right and continue along the riverbank path. In due course this winds to the left, climbs and reaches the road, crossing a few stiles on the way. (The bridleway does follow the access road but this last stretch along the Mells river is a footpath only.) At the road turn left, uphill, to see the village and church; turn right downhill to reach the bridge and continue the walk.

2. Great Elm is a most pretty place with a Norman church, Tudor rectory and 17th century manor farm all facing a little green. Down by the bridge is a picture-postcard scene with a lake, ducks, boat house and collection of ornamental trees. The grounds of Bridge House have hosted an annual Music Festival since 1987, founded in memory of Peter Wishart. On the far (south) bank of the Mells river the woodlands rise steeply. This is the site of an Iron Age fort called Tedbury Camp.

3. Those neither wishing to climb a long ascending path, nor to end their circular walk along a road, could do worse than return to Mells back along the same track. Otherwise the route lies across the bridge and through the gate. Two directions are shown by footpath arrow discs; straight on along the riverbank and half-left uphill. The former leads to a single-track railway line and bends right to wander through the woods. The latter is the route to choose. This path climbs steadily under the trees and then levels off to follow the top of the woodland. This is another pleasant stretch. The rail track below, to the right, serves only a local quarry and can thus be ignored. Only a few train loads run along daily. Eventually the path meets the Mells to Frome road. Turn right. The walk back is about a mile and there is a verge for much of the way.

PLACES OF INTEREST NEARBY
The Rode Bird Gardens are 6 miles north-east of Mells, a collection of tropical birds being kept in the grounds of now demolished Rode Manor (telephone: 01373 830326). A few miles north of there is *Farleigh Hungerford Castle*, ruins of a 14th century fortified manor now held by English Heritage (telephone: 01225 754026).

THE RIVER BRUE AT BRUTON

In this well timbered landscape, several fast-flowing rivers, such as the Frome, the Stour and the Brue, have cut deep valleys creating a very attractive, undulating countryside. This walk from the historic town of Bruton follows the upper Brue valley to the hamlet of Cole and lovely little Pitcombe and returns near Bruton's ancient Dovecot. The paths used are clear but some gradients are encountered.

The stepping stones at Bruton

From Frome southwards to Wincanton, and beyond, a great forest once covered the Somerset-Wiltshire-Dorset borderlands. This was called Selwood and for much of its history, from Saxon to Tudor times, it was used as a royal hunting forest. Bruton is a very attractive, stone-built little place of great historic importance. There was a Saxon mint here and, in the 12th century, an Augustinian priory was founded on the southern edge of town. Sadly little of this ecclesiastical complex survives – except for the Pigeon Tower, or Dovecot, that stands on top of a nearby hill (now owned by the National Trust). The church of St Mary stands on the edge of the old priory site. It has Saxon foundations but the present structure dates largely from the 14th and 15th centuries. Today Bruton's townscape is dominated by educational buildings, there being several independent boys' and girls' schools here. The oldest and most well-known of these is King's School, first endowed in the 16th century. This occupies many separate buildings dating from the 16th to 20th century and accounts for much of the social activity of the town. Sexey's School (founded in the 19th century) also is distributed between many sites. The original core was the 17th century Sexey's Hospital building, which is arranged around a quadrangle.

There is no shortage of establishments in Bruton for refreshment opportunities. The Royal Oak Inn in Combe Street prides itself on its range of real ales, which includes a weekly guest beer and its very own brewed Sharpe's Brue. It is a large, spacious inn with a large bar room, function facilities, skittle alley and accommodation. Daily specials are written up on blackboards above the bar counter and there is always a 'Kids Menu'. Snacks and meals range from sandwiches and salads to grills and steaks, from fish dishes to pasta bakes. Telephone: 01749 812215.

- **HOW TO GET THERE:** Bruton stands 4 miles north of Wincanton and 6 miles south-east of Shepton Mallet. It is on the A359 Sparkford-Frome road.
- **PARKING:** Bruton has narrow streets but spaces can be found away from the main roads. There is a free car park off Combe Street, behind the Blue Ball Inn.
- **LENGTH OF THE WALK:** 3½ miles. Map: OS Landranger 183 Yeovil & Frome (GR 684349).

THE WALK

1. From Combe Street walk westwards along the High Street past the Sun Inn and Castle Inn on the right, and a very inviting Coffee House on the left. At the far end, the main road dips downhill and bears left. Do not follow the path indicated up Trendle Lane (straight ahead) which is part of the Leland Trail and goes to Wyke Champflower. Instead follow the road round the corner and then turn right up Tower Hill, between a petrol station and garage workshop. Soon you will see a bridleway signpost pointing to Wyke Lane and Cole. The Mill on the Brue Activity Centre is ahead.

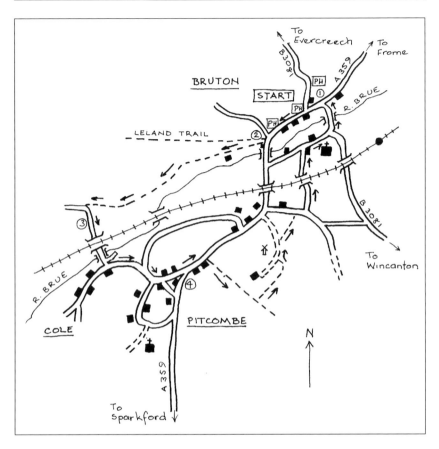

2. Follow the bridleway up to the main building of the Activity Centre. Immediately before the wall of its surrounding garden, turn left through a gateway. The route now skirts the (private) buildings and contours along the valley slope. The river Brue is down to the left. Walking through the grounds of the Centre (popular with school parties throughout the year) head west: first across the top of the playing fields, then alongside a hedgerow and close to an old stone ruin. Past some wood-and-rope climbing apparatus you soon reach a gate. Through this the bridleway continues along the top of woodland, the river now being quite close. Two more gates bring you to an attractive group of buildings (private) evidently once an old mill complex. The route skirts above this hamlet and continues along the valley side. Keeping roughly parallel to the river down to the left, but gaining height gradually, aim for the top corner in each of the next two

Bruton Dovecot

fields. Soon you will see the railway line down below as well as the Brue. In due course you will reach a gate that takes you through onto a country lane. Turn left to follow this downhill.

3. Keeping to the lane, go under the railway bridge, over the river and bear right to reach the hamlet of Cole. At the T junction turn left and continue on to Pitcombe (ignoring a narrow lane that goes sharp left on your way). The circular walk now keeps bearing left as it climbs uphill in a curve, eventually joining the main A359 road. Those with time should stay awhile and explore Pitcombe (turning right and downhill at the first junction). This is a lovely little spot with a scatter of old cottages strung along a series of bends, as the road meanders around the course of the lost Somerset and Dorset railway line. The viaduct is still there, offering shelter to farm machinery.

4. Walk along the A359 towards Bruton, but not for long. On the right-hand side, just past a line of detached houses, is a kissing gate and footpath signpost pointing to Lower Shepton. Follow the route indicated, uphill along a wide trackway across a field. At the top of the climb continue along a concrete track for 100 yards, until you reach a stile on the left. The footpath leads along by a hedgerow, over another stile and onwards to the far corner of the second field. Bruton Dovecot will be seen ahead. The stile in the corner takes you onto a main trackway. Turn right, downhill, past a radio mast, which is over to the left. Before you reach the bottom of the hill cross the stile that you will see on the right. This path takes you across a field down to another stile, thence through a small thicket, over a footbridge and up beside some back gardens. At the road turn right to the next junction and then sharp left. Beside some playing fields (beyond which is the Dovecot) you soon cross the railway line and turn right for Bruton church.

PLACES OF INTEREST NEARBY
Hadspen Garden, 3 miles south-west of Bruton, is an Edwardian estate that includes a restored walled garden, a woodland of specimen trees and a nursery (telephone: 01963 50939). Only 6 miles eastward, across into Wiltshire, is the famous National Trust property of *Stourhead House and Garden* which should not be missed. Alfred's Tower, on the Stourhead estate, offers extensive views (telephone: 01747 841152).

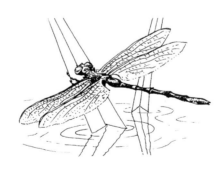

WALK 20

THE CAM MEADOWS AND CADBURY CASTLE

South-eastern Somerset has a landscape of broad meadows and steep rolling hills, of narrow winding lanes and unspoilt villages. It is a most beautiful yet unexplored corner of the county. From Sparkford, this walk across the valley of the river Cam offers a taste of this scenery using easy-to-follow paths and quiet country roads, visiting the pretty settlements of Little Weston, South Cadbury, Sutton Montis and Weston Bampfylde for good measure. From the top of Cadbury Castle, for those who undertake the climb, there is a spectacular view.

The River Cam at Sparkford

Sparkford, where the walk begins, is a slightly sprawling village, now thankfully by-passed by the A303. Here and there are some attractive cottages, and the church, which stands at the southern end, boasts a fine Perpendicular tower. A memorial in the south chapel remembers eight local men who died in the Great War, the poignancy heightened

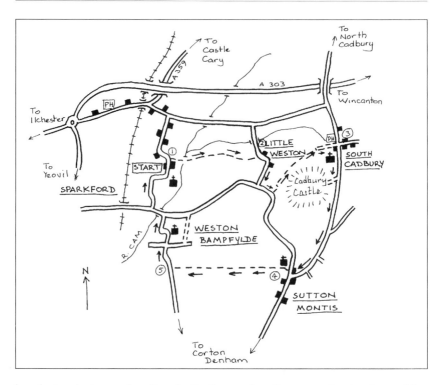

by their photographs. South Cadbury, 2 miles east, is dominated by Cadbury Castle which towers above the cluster of cottages. It is a pretty village with a good mixture of buildings, including 17th century Castle Farm and 18th century South Cadbury House. The church dates back to the 14th century but was largely modernised in Victorian times. Cadbury Castle itself is a wooded eminence that rises to 500 feet. The Iron Age embankments on top enclose 18 acres and once contained not so much a fort but a Celtic town. This was sacked by the Romans but was later rebuilt to enable the Britons to defend themselves against the invading Saxons. Legend tells us that this site was the original Camelot, King Arthur's fortress, and the place was certainly an important stronghold at the time the mythical Arthur is thought to have lived. An old trackway once linked South Cadbury with Glastonbury, this being called on old maps 'King Arthur's Hunting Causeway'.

The Sparkford Inn is a freehouse selling Wadworth and Otter ales and offering a wide range of excellent meals from bar snacks to large main courses such as steak and kidney pie, faggots, and curry. Daily specials are listed on a blackboard and there is a separate carvery. It is a large building with open-plan bar rooms, low ceilings and a dark cosy atmosphere. Telephone: 01963 440218.

- **HOW TO GET THERE:** Sparkford is 7 miles west of Wincanton and 8 miles north-east of Yeovil, next to the A303.
- **PARKING:** Vehicles can be left anywhere in the village provided no obstruction is caused.
- **LENGTH OF THE WALK:** 5 miles. Map: OS Landranger 183 Yeovil & Frome (GR 609257).

THE WALK

1. The route begins just 100 yards north of the church. Next to a line of garages is a gate, stile and footpath sign pointing east. Little Weston is ¾ mile away. A clear path leads across a rough field to a stile and footbridge over the river Cam. Walk across this and continue straight on (ignoring the gate and path to the right, which enters private land). Keeping the hedgerow to your right proceed to the next stile and little footbridge. Thereafter bear left and aim for the top corner of a large field. Cadbury Castle should be ahead. Continue over the next stile and across the next field, keeping the hedgerow to your right. After the next stile turn right to cut across the corner of a field and then (after another stile) left. Now the hedgerow should be to your left. Across a double stile and over a ditch aim across the last field to the right of a red-brick pair of houses. The road at Little Weston is soon reached. Turn right.

2. Walk through the quiet and pretty hamlet of Little Weston and up the road to a T junction where you turn left. At the next bend is a footpath signpost. The route now follows the Leland Trail. This long-distance path through South Somerset links King Alfred's Tower, on the Wiltshire border, with Ham Hill near Montacute. It was opened in 1989 and is named after John Leland, the 16th century scholar who travelled widely in this part of England. From the bend in the road turn sharp left, to walk alongside a hedgerow for 50 yards, and then climb a stile to continue in the same direction, now with the hedgerow on your right. Cadbury Castle should be up to your right. Several stiles further will bring you to a clear trackway. This you follow all the way to South Cadbury, emerging onto the road at the Red Lion. Turn right.

3. Those climbing Cadbury Castle will find the ascending trackway soon after the church. The effort is well worthwhile. Apart from the interest of the fortifications themselves, the views from the summit are wonderful, especially to the north over the Somerset Levels towards the Mendips. The circular walk continues along the road all the way to Sutton Montis, skirting the lower slopes of Cadbury Castle. It is a very quiet road and the hills all around make for a very pleasant stroll. At the T junction in the village, turn right for the church. This is an attractive building with a 13th century tower, 19th century nave and a curious classical-style porch.

4. The route, for the second time, now follows the Leland Trail. The footpath signpost stands at the churchyard gate and points to Queen Camel. Follow the direction indicated across the graveyard and then, over a stile, half left. The way is clear: almost straight, it runs diagonally across several fields and each stile boasts an arrow disc. Ahead, in the distance, are the Cam meadows and, beyond these, the Somerset Levels. In due course a final stile, deep in a field corner, takes you onto the road, just south of Weston Bampfylde.

5. The last section is northward, along the lane that winds through this unspoilt village where farms and cottages cluster around a succession of bends. The church has an interesting tower, with an octagonal top – a later addition to a 13th century base. After crossing the river Cam keep right at the junction. Soon Sparkford church is reached.

PLACES OF INTEREST NEARBY
Sparkford is the home of the Haynes Publishing Group, famous for its motorcar manuals. In 1985 John Haynes founded the *Sparkford Motor Museum* just north of the village. This has become very popular and includes various exhibits, a display track, bookshop and cafe (telephone: 01963 46804). Near Podimore, 5 miles west of Sparkford, is Lytes Cary, a 15th century mansion owned by the National Trust (telephone: 01985 843600).